New York University Series In Education and Socialization in American History

THE REVOLUTIONARY COLLEGE
American Presbyterian Higher Education, 1707-1837
Howard Miller

THE CLASSLESS PROFESSION
American Schoolmen of the Nineteenth Century
Paul H. Mattingly

The publication of this work has been aided by a grant
from the Andrew W. Mellon Foundation

Alice Freeman Palmer (center left) with some Wellesley students, 1885.
Courtesy of Wellesley College Archives.

COLLEGIATE WOMEN

Domesticity and Career in Turn-of-the-Century America

Roberta Frankfort

New York · NEW YORK UNIVERSITY PRESS · 1977

Library of Congress Catalog Card Number: 76-53614
ISBN: 0-8147-2563-5

Library of Congress Cataloging in Publication Data

Frankfort, Roberta, 1945-
  Collegiate women.

  Includes bibliographical references and index.
  1. Higher education of women—United States—History—
Addresses, essays, lectures.   2. Women college teachers—
United States—History—Addresses, essays, lectures.
3. Women—United States—History—Addresses, essays,
lectures.   I. Title.
LC1756.F7   376'.65'0973   76-53614
ISBN 0-8147-2563-5

Manufactured in the United States of America

To Lewis

Contents

Acknowledgments

In a real sense the major character in this book—Jane Addams—almost does not appear in it. My reading of her book, *Twenty Years at Hull House*, was the start of this study. In particular, I focused on her aspirations to go to Smith College and her experiences at what was then Rockford Seminary. I wished to examine in historical perspective problems of "the snare of preparation" that she discussed, in order to see if her peers faced similar dilemmas and to determine how unusual her work at Hull House really was. Ultimately, I found her representative with respect to the formulation of her problems but unique in her solutions.

This study represents the last in a series of revisions. It originated in my doctoral work in the Department of Historic and Philosophic Foundations of Education at New York University. The seminars and independent study sessions in that department offered me a solid foundation for intellectual growth. I am most indebted to Paul Mattingly, whose incisive criticisms and interpretive suggestions have been crucial to the progress of this manuscript from dissertation to book. In addition, I especially appreciate the suggestions of Allan Horlick of New York University, who helped shape my doctoral study, and Berenice Fisher, also of New York University, who spent much time with me in textual analysis and offered her insights for revision.

Many library staffs have assisted me in the course of my research.

Those at Bryn Mawr College, Wellesley College, and the Berg Collection at the New York Public Library were particularly helpful in enabling me to locate pertinent materials.

It would be impossible to mention all colleagues and friends who have willingly and even eagerly permitted me to sort out some of my thoughts by talking them through or who have read parts of the various manuscripts and made suggestions. I would like to thank in particular Rose Mukerji, my colleague at Brooklyn College, who offered guidance and much needed encouragement.

Neither my dissertation nor this study would have been completed without the constant support of my immediate family, especially my husband, Lewis.

Foreword

In the past decade and a half American historians attempted a new integration of techniques and interpretations developed by their colleagues in the humanities and social sciences. This interdisciplinary sharing produced a "New History" which is at once more instructive about current American dilemmas and more historical in its concern for the dynamics of past change.

This Series, Education and Socialization in American History, fosters the most recent, significant studies of cultural change within this new historical orientation. The agents of change here are no longer depersonalized forces, exemplary figures directing critical events, or heroic dramas of battles with clear victories. Nor is change itself some vague happening which somehow affects the multiple public sectors of living and thinking. By contrast here, the historical process of socialization becomes a varied interaction of definable social groups and their leaders. These groups become worthy of serious study because of their intellectual and behavioral response to major questions about the American past. Through their organizations, particularly their schools, one can sort out and comprehend the relationships between detailed historical experiences and those preeminent questions which have shaped the American past.

The Series has given special attention to education, since there in the transmission of social values and intellectual skills societies define themselves historically. All of the contributors have tried to conceive education and socialization broadly. They have consciously interpreted the creation of pertinent institutions and their value systems as reciprocal determinants of educational history. The breadth and depth of these studies lie in the interconnections drawn between the detailed routines of group life and the collective mentalities of an era. Historical interpretation itself has adopted a more aggressive responsibility and sophistication. So often in the past the meaning and significance of events and documents became mere organizational problems, which grouped data indiscriminately under confusing and superficial abstractions. Here scholars have begun with such notions as professional training, the colonial college, progressive schools and the like, not as organizational but as historically problematic ideas, concepts with different meanings over time. The significance of past ideas do not speak for themselves any more than do historical facts; both require interpretation and ongoing scrutiny. Textual analysis has a fascination for historians of this Series equal to this appreciation of quantitative and demographic analysis. Together these varied methodologies permit new interpretations from the interactions between institutions and their ideologies.

There is in a sense something old as well as something new in these social and educational histories. From the best of both the contributing scholars hope for something beyond entertainment and inspiration. They seek rather to illuminate those dilemmas and historical tensions which each generation must rework according to its inheritance: the problems of failure as well as success, of the basic conditions of life as well as the strategic manipulations of public policy, of the ongoing stratification of social groups as well as the more obvious rituals of American life. To grasp the historicity of these responses is the only advantage of retrospect; it is most certainly also the first necessary stage for any real comprehension of present-day confusions. This Series has committed itself to the refinement and reinterpretation of these key historical problems.

Since schools are never fully pawns or panaceas, the Series historians have taken stock of education's shifting importance in different historical periods. The histories go beyond chronicle, strictly speaking, and focus upon the various uses of schooling in a broader cultural perspective. In the understanding of that perspective, in its scope and detail, these studies propose to further both a new history and a higher learning.

Paul H. Mattingly
Series Editor

Introduction

The nineteenth-century idealization of family life, which called for the morally superior mother and wife to remain at the hearthside in order to purify her family, and thus her country, has received much attention from historians and those studying present-day women's roles. The questions of when this ideal emerged and why it was so widely accepted have been and will be debated; but it is agreed that domesticity has been a point of departure for women since its genesis. The ethos surrounding this domestic ideal shaped the lives of women who subscribed fully to it and practically assured ostracism for women who chose to reject it entirely. Those who were ambivalent were perhaps the most immersed in it, for many sought—and still seek—their whole lives to find a balance between home life and outside interests.

This domestic ideal was certainly by 1830 an extraordinarily powerful set of assumptions, dictating that the woman with her mysterious "life-giving powers which defied man's comprehension" [1] had the sanctified duty to create a home that would bring men and children closer to God. From a twentieth-century perspective the whole notion seems offensive to many involved with winning equal rights for women. And historians intent on defining domesticity have stated that the ideal may have elevated women spiritually, but it simultaneously degraded them,[2] for it dictated that these higher sensibilities made women "wholly unsuited to the rough world outside the home. This was just as well, because women were largely responsible for the Family—the principal adornment of Christian civilization, and the bedrock upon which society rested."[3] Nineteenth-century women have come to be widely viewed as victims of oppression, subtle or otherwise.[4]

The ideal of domesticity required propagation. The literature for women in the nineteenth century did not question the merits of a domestic life; indeed, it elaborated very specifically upon ways of conforming to it. Manuals and magazines instructed women on proper household techniques and childrearing practices. And schools for girls—particularly academies and seminaries—provided a context where social expectation of acceptable behavior for women and the education that they received were very directly correlated. Those who headed such schools were intent upon presenting a coherent picture of the elements that produced a sound and virtuous character; they wished to avoid any ambiguities or confusions about proper feminine activity.

It is evident that the domestic ideal itself did not change nearly as much as women's reactions to it, particularly in the latter part of the nineteenth century. The women who responded most vehemently and negatively were those political radicals who fought for suffrage and sought to eradicate the sometimes subtle legal distinctions that forced women into a state of bondage in their marriages. These women, who began to alter the connotations of domesticity, have received the most attention from historians. But by the late nineteenth century other women began to see higher education as a way to challenge, within an educational institution, some of the tenets surrounding the domestic ideal.

The responses of women in education to domesticity cannot be easily categorized. Unlike radical feminists involved in political struggle, women in education did not have clearly defined targets or goals. Their milieu—women's higher education—was a new phenomenon and was viewed by some as a vehicle for dramatic change in women's occupational as well as psychological states. Yet higher education also could be seen as an extension of the generally conservative secondary schools. This study focuses upon the ways in which certain educated women evaluated and used higher educational institutions. It necessarily involves the dynamic interplay between notions of domesticity and educational institutions that encroached on domestic concerns. To what extent did women pay homage to the family ideal, and how did this affect their activities and institutional attachments? And did this relationship between ideology and institutional arrangement affect the career patterns of the students that attended these institutions? Through the study of the careers of specific presidents of women's colleges and the careers of the students that they tried to influence, relationships can be seen between education and later life, between domestic ideals inculcated through education and eventual career patterns. It is important to note that I am not suggesting a causal relation between the ideologies of the presidents and career patterns of the graduates. Rather, it seems clear that both the ideas and the patterns arose during the proliferation of the female college and that they held each other together. In some way the rhetoric of the presidents served to reassure parents and incoming students about the priorities in their institutions rather than to alter dramatically the aspirations of the undergraduates.

I am also concerned in this study with change. How did the responses to domesticity, and concomitantly, the specific institutions discussed, as well as the careers of the graduates, change? And, finally, did these different responses ultimately alter the ranges of the domestic ideal itself?

Nineteenth-century women in higher education were highly visible. The public at large was curious to discover whether these women would develop behavioral as well as intellectual qualities that their male counterparts possessed. Indeed, college-educated women often viewed their institutional affiliations as stigmas since they might exhaust much of their energies trying to prove that college had left their femininity intact. Thus, in studying women's responses to the domestic ideal, it is useful to begin with a precollegiate woman whose reactions to domesticity were not affected by her associations with a college. The earlier responses help to measure the degree of change that actually occurred. In addition, the challenges of college women did not arise in a vacuum. Women educators had set certain patterns of responses to domesticity, and their styles affected the way women dealt with the conflict later in the nineteenth century.

I begin, then, with Elizabeth Palmer Peabody, who, like Alice Freeman Palmer and Martha Carey Thomas, was not chosen because she was necessarily representative of her time or because her activities were necessarily typical of other educated women of her generation. Rather, her life provides rich material for studying relationships between notions of domesticity and career. In vivid contrast to most college women, Peabody's institutional affiliations were often loosely structured and ephemeral; this seemed to be intentional and useful, given her sensitivity to the conflict between passivity and aggressive behavior (defined in terms of prevailing domestic ideals).

Unlike Peabody, Alice Freeman Palmer's visibility was insured when she assumed the presidency of Wellesley College. But her position, which was powerful and demanded rigor and aggressiveness, was incompatible with her stated feelings about proper spheres for women. Her conflict was poignantly dramatized in her difficult decision to leave Wellesley College and marry, which is described in the first chapter. Martha Carey Thomas, however, had no such feelings of ambivalence, particularly during the first part of her tenure as president of Bryn Mawr College; she had a strong commitment to higher education as providing a path to real alternatives to domesticity. The ways in which these two women perceived roles and careers of educated women are discussed in Chapters Two and Three; their translation of ideology into policy is compared in Chapter Four.

Carey Thomas's rhetoric undergoes a change about 1910. Her previous steadfast commitment to the unmarried female scholar gave way to a reluctant acceptance of the possibility that marriage and career could be combined and that careers other than those connected with academia—notably social work—might be pursued by college-educated women. This rhetorical change led me to investigate possible shifts in career patterns of college graduates that may have influenced Thomas's public pronouncements. After compiling statistics about marriage rates, occupations, and advanced study for graduates of Wellesley and Bryn Mawr from the years 1889 to 1918, I did find a very substantial shift—particularly in the statistics for Bryn Mawr—around the time that Thomas's speeches began to show some evident change. Thus, after examining in Chapter Four differences in Wellesley and Bryn Mawr statistics from 1889 to 1908—when numerical patterns seemed to be clearly correlated with the variation of the two institutional emphases—I begin in Chapter Five to document and discuss this change. I found that by 1908 more Bryn Mawr and Wellesley students were marrying, although the change for the former group was far more dramatic. Moreover, fewer Bryn Mawr women pursued occupations upon graduation and fewer Wellesley and Bryn Mawr graduates went on to further study. Indeed, statistics for graduates of the two colleges, which had previously varied rather strikingly, were approaching each other by 1908. The data are quite revealing, for they seem to indicate that the infant female colleges, which had begun to produce a substantial number of women who did not conform to domestic precepts, graduated, after a few short years, women who were more inclined to embrace a life centered around the home.

In order to determine whether patterns discussed with reference to Bryn Mawr and Wellesley hold true in a wider arena and also to identify reasons for the change, I focus, in Chapter Six, upon the Association of

Collegiate Alumnae (ACA), which was, in the late nineteenth and early twentieth centuries, a very active organization comprising women college graduates. Upon examination of speeches given in annual conventions and articles appearing in ACA publications, I found that determination to prove feminine scholarly prowess is replaced with talk about reconciling domesticity and a college education. New careers for women in such fields as hygiene, social work, and home economy became the bridges linking these formerly polarized ideals.

The reasons for these shifts can be found only partially in the internal conflicts of educated women—conflicts that, for many, become resolved when science and resulting professionalism bring a new status to housekeeping and philanthropic work. It is necessary, of course, to examine changes within particular institutions and groups of individuals in a larger social context. In the case of the ACA, an interesting phenomenon occurs about the time of the statistical and rhetorical changes: outsiders—mostly academic and government men—begin to speak before the ACA for the first time, and they consistently encourage and praise new directions in women's higher education. The "outside," so to speak, reaches in to a heretofore exclusionary institution; the kinds of comments that these men make reveal that wider societal uses have been found for educated women; this acceptance of college women by members of a group that had, twenty years before, largely shunned the whole idea of female higher education, was part of a general feeling that the limits of domesticity might be expanded from the home to the unsanitary city with its growing number of dependent people. College women might work to alleviate the more inhumane effects of industrialization and urbanization. The comments also reveal—in a narrower sense—that the success of new, specialized courses for women in such fields as home economy and hygiene served the purposes of some academic men, who saw these courses first as a way of segregating the increasing population of women in coeducational institutions, and, second, as a means of legitimizing their own drives toward promoting undergraduate education that stressed professional utility.

In the Epilogue, I return to a discussion of an individual woman. Unlike Elizabeth Peabody, Alice Palmer, or Carey Thomas, Ellen H. Richards is I think representative. Her career was unusual, but her views seem to epitomize the apparent consensus discussed in the last chapter. For Richards domestic science was a way to bring professional status to traditional woman's work—to enable women to manage effectively their own sphere almost as if it were a new industry. In reality, however, this "professionalism" never really brought women a higher status; on the contrary, in some real way it made them less powerful than a previous generation had been. The domestic ideology was now enshrined in a much more specialized and hence more controlled arena.

The first twenty or so years of women's colleges—at least with reference to Bryn Mawr and Wellesley—are remarkable in that the variations between the institutions were so visible. Bryn Mawr in particular was a promising alternative to the kind of education women were receiving in academies and seminaries and in some of the early female colleges.[5] Perhaps the newness of both the colleges themselves and the general institutional form allowed the flexibility and the dynamic quality of the interactions between ideology, institutional arrangement, and resulting career patterns. The maturation of the institutions seemed to assure a degree of conformity that was not present before. Both the involvement of outsiders and the increased communications between the colleges (particularly through the Association of Collegiate Alumnae) contributed to a greater homogeneity. This process is certainly not unique to women's colleges. But it seems, in this period at least, to have taken its toll on the ease with which college-educated women could choose life styles not sanctioned by domesticity.

NOTES

1. William O'Neill, *Everyone Was Brave: The Rise and Fall of Feminism in America* (Chicago, 1969), p. 7.

2. Barbara Welter, "The Cult of True Womanhood: 1820-1860," *American Quarterly* 18 (Summer 1966): 162. This article is widely quoted, for it is the only real attempt to discuss aspects of this domesticity cult. Welter's work is descriptive, and she primarily reviewed women's magazines, gift annuals, and religious literature in order to isolate categories of attributes.

3. O'Neill, p. 7.

4. In a recent article entitled "The Female World of Love and Ritual: Relations between Women in Nineteenth Century America" [*SIGNS Journal of Women in Culture and Society* 1 (Autumn 1975)] Carroll Smith Rosenberg points out that many women drew sustenance from this domestic life, "bounded by home, church, and the institution of visiting—that endless trooping of women to each others' homes for social purposes" (p. 10). Rosenberg further points out: "Women, however, did not form an isolated and oppressed subcategory in male society. Their letters and diaries indicate that women's sphere had an essential integrity and dignity that grew out of women's shared experiences and mutual affection and that, despite the profound changes which affected American social structure and institutions between the 1760s and the 1870s, retained a constancy and predictability" (pp. 9-10).

5. See Thomas Woody, *History of Women's Education in the United States*, Vols.

1 and 2 (New York, 1929), for a discussion of curricula of academies, seminaries, and the early female colleges. Woody's volumes on women's education are really the starting point for any work on female education in the United States before World War I. The work is full of facts and figures gleaned primarily from records of institutions, general and educational periodicals—including the Commissioner of Education's *Reports*—as well as general works on women's education that were available. All of these sources are listed at the back of the volumes. The volumes, though, lack any interpretive framework and are therefore helpful only in the mass of information and sources that they provide.

COLLEGIATE WOMEN

Domesticity
and Career in
Turn-of-the-Century
America

PROLOGUE

Elizabeth Palmer Peabody:
A Precollegiate Woman

Elizabeth Palmer Peabody's life spanned almost the entire nineteenth century—she was born in 1804 and died in 1894. But her prime source of identification was with the precollegiate woman whose self-education instilled a great passion for knowledge and who, according to Thomas Wentworth Higginson, was always involved in countless causes. Institutional commitments were short-lived as the precollegiate woman scurried from one attachment to another, looking for outlets in which to concentrate her abundant energies.

Higginson affectionately tells an amusing story about the last time he met Miss Peabody, who was then nearly 90 years old. There was a horrible snowstorm in Boston. Higginson was out on the streets when he saw Miss Peabody stumbling and falling in the snow. As soon as she caught sight of him, she immediately inquired about enlisting his assistance in the case of Sarah Winnemucca, an Indian half-breed who was trying to start a school. Miss Peabody was on her way to speak to someone who might possibly contribute to her latest—and final—cause.[1]

The cause to which Elizabeth Peabody attached the most importance was education, and her activities ranged from working with Bronson Alcott in his Temple School, to selling Bem's charts (historical tables for memorizing dates), to promoting kindergartens based on the principles of Fredrich Froebel, to starting numerous schools of her own. She

3

attributed her intense involvement to her mother who, she claimed, prepared her for the teaching vocation: "There I was born in 1804—being as it were prenatally educated for the profession that has been the passionate pursuit of my life." [2] Her mother, Elizabeth Peabody, seems to have been an unusually strong, insistent woman; she instilled in her child the belief that teaching was the noblest occupation for American women. Because of their higher moral sensibilities, they were eminently qualified to be guardians of the young:

> But she [her mother] was not censorious of individuals nor wanting in tenderness, and referred to their faults so invariably to bad education or no education, that when I entered on this vocation myself—a vocation for which she educated me, considering it the highest and the proper activity of every American woman who loved her country—moral education became to my mind the essence of all education.[3]

Aside from giving Elizabeth Peabody a thorough education and inspiring her to become an educator, her mother provided a strong role model from which Elizabeth seemed to draw much sustenance. The male members of her family, her father and three younger brothers, were all weak and ineffectual. Her father was never able to support the family without help from his indomitable wife, who supplemented her husband's income by running schools. Two of her brothers were expelled from Harvard, and all three went from one occupation to another without success. The nervously energetic Peabody women, including Elizabeth's two younger sisters, took over the family affairs.

It is no wonder, then, that Elizabeth Peabody acquired an aggressive demeanor which, combined with a general neglect of her appearance, was offensive to many who met her as a young woman. Bronson Alcott, who first knew her when she was supporting her family by running a school for the children of Boston's intelligentsia and was attempting to draw closer to Boston's transcendental circle, described her unfavorably. He thought her extremely negligent, mostly because of her seemingly studied and artificial manners. In addition, he felt that she failed in her attempt to be original by being too much man and too little woman in her familiarity and freedom.[4]

Bronson Alcott's response to Elizabeth Peabody was not unusual; nor was it difficult to understand in a society that was beginning to subscribe to the domesticity cult, whose advocates idealized sweet, submissive, pure femininity. The woman who ventured from the home to the cosmopolitan, intellectual world composed mainly of men was immediately subject to hostility. But within a few years of Elizabeth Peabody's appearance in the public Boston arena, her presence aroused little antagonism. Indeed, by the end of her life she was regarded with affection and amusement by many who either knew her or had heard of her activities. When part of Henry James's work, *The Bostonians,* appeared in the February 4, 1885, issue of *Century Magazine,* people were struck by certain similarities between the fictional Miss Birdseye and Elizabeth P. Peabody. Miss Birdseye, according to the author, is a veteran philanthropist—weary, battered, and simpleminded. She is sympathetic, pathetic, picturesque, and at the same time grotesque with her ci-devant transcendental tendencies.[5] William James wrote an indignant letter to his brother protesting the seemingly slanderous portrait. But Henry replied that he intended no such defamation of Miss Peabody's character. In fact, he said, his only scruple involved some touch about Miss Birdseye's spectacles—he remembered that Miss Peabody's were everywhere except at the bridge of her nose. He ends the letter by saying that Miss Birdseye, though subordinate, is the best figure in the novel. Then Henry James writes to his brother: "so . . . I find this charge on the subject of Miss Peabody a very cold douche indeed."[6]

Henry James's intentions can be debated. But the fact that many readers made the identification is significant. Elizabeth Peabody had managed to defy constraints of proper feminine deportment in order to attend to her many causes. In an age when much controversy surrounded the women who pursued a career outside the home, a satirical response from those who found her most ungenteel was at least more acceptable than a harsh reaction. Miss Peabody trooped through Boston unscathed by the criticism that accompanied other women such as Margaret Fuller, who traveled in similar circles but whose activities aroused deep animosity in Boston society, outside of a small group of intellectuals.

Elizabeth Peabody's ability to remain unhampered by indictments of her work was partially due to her lack of interest in issues touching on the conflict between the domesticity ideal and aggressive behavior in women. She ignored entirely—until very late in her life—the activities of women fighting for political rights. Her writings are extremely scanty on the whole subject of feminism. In one of her rare statements on women's rights, she said that she was surprised when she read the first call of a convention of women's rights in 1837, for she felt that women could and were allowed to take any course for which they were fit.[7] When asked to sign the convention call, she refused, replying that she would change the title women's rights to women's duties, "which if thoroughly understood by them, would involve their having correlative rights, without anybody's disputing or hindering."[8]

Her response to "them" was clearly intended to be ambiguous. She avoided any possibility of involving herself in so inflammable an issue by denying that a woman's problem even existed. Respective functions of man and woman are complementary, she replied, while refusing to acknowledge her own ventures from the home. By 1837, when the convention call came, Elizabeth Peabody had published a book and several articles, was a widely respected teacher, and was intimately associated with some of the more eccentric of the Boston intellectuals, such as Ralph Waldo Emerson and Bronson Alcott.

Her association with Alcott was an interesting one, for it shows Miss Peabody's avoidance of controversial issues—issues that might potentially place her in the public eye and disrupt the calm with which she pursued her activities. The particular incident, so revealing of her behavior in the face of conflict, had its beginnings when Peabody and Alcott—who had recovered from his initial dislike for Elizabeth Peabody—began to talk of the latter's ideas on teaching. Peabody was impressed by Alcott's conversation method, through which he intended to help bring out children's spiritual thoughts. And, as was so characteristic of her, "she earnestly desired closer association with the man whose mind at the moment she most admired." [9]

Peabody became Alcott's assistant teacher at the Temple School with whatever compensation he could afford. At that time she was widely reputed to be a very capable teacher; it is therefore significant that she accepted Bronson Alcott as her superior, procured students for his school, served gladly as his assistant, and took elaborate notes on his teaching method. She undertook the task willingly, believing that Alcott's teaching philosophy was superior even to her own: "I am vain enough to say that you are the only one I ever saw who, I soberly thought, surpassed myself in the general conception of this divinest of arts." [10]

Record of a School, which details Alcott's teaching methods, was published in 1835. Interspersed between Elizabeth Peabody's attempts at objective recording are a few personal opinions of Alcott's methods. Practically all of these were positive; when she did raise an objection, she often found that after intensive observation and discussion with Alcott, her reservations were overcome. In one section she criticizes Alcott for unwittingly leading the children into his own direction of thought during the conversations: "I generally agree with the views that Mr. Alcott brings out from his pupils; but in this instance I am inclined to think that he unconsciously led them into his own views; by contradistinguishing mercy and justice." [11] This statement anticipated some later public criticism of Alcott.

But the *Record* was well received. For the most part, readers of such magazines as the *Western Messenger* and the *Christian Examiner* were urged to read Miss Peabody's *Record of a School.* One reviewer said: "By those who take a deep interest in the much canvassed topic of education, if also in any degree inclined to transcendentalism, or to a more spiritual philosophy than generally prevails, this book will be read and studied with great eagerness and satisfaction." [12]

By the end of 1835, however, the close relationship between Alcott and Peabody began to wither, primarily because she disapproved of Alcott's conversations with the children on the gospels, in which such delicate subjects as the birth of Christ were discussed in an unorthodox manner. One such conversation was recorded by Sophia Peabody, who was substituting for her sister that day. Alcott found that the children knew nothing about birth. He wished them to understand that the deliverance of the spirit is primary; the physical is only a sign of the spiritual birth. In carefully chosen words he said:

> . . . the deliverance of the spirit is the first thing. . . . The physiological facts, sometimes referred to, are only a sign of the spiritual birth. You have seen the rose opening from the seed with the assistance of the atmosphere. This is the birth of the rose. It typified the bringing forth of the spirit by pain and labor and patience. . . . And a mother suffers when she has a child. When she is going to have a child she gives up her body to God and He works upon it in a mysterious way, and, with her aid, brings forth the child's Spirit in a little Body of its own; and when it has come she is blissful.[13]

Peabody left the school in the spring of 1836, telling her sister Mary that private quarrels and Mr. Alcott's general lack of humility [14] were the reasons. But in reality she left because she feared a public barrage of criticism over Alcott's conversations with the children on the gospels, which he was considering for publication. The whispers in Boston's "best families" were growing louder, and she did not wish to entangle herself in the impending uproar. When, during the summer of 1836, Alcott revealed definite intentions to publish the conversations, Peabody was upset. Although she had left the school, she had recorded many of the conversations, and she feared that she would be implicated. Thus she wrote a long letter to Alcott asking that he make certain stipulations "that would place her in the role of passive, irresponsible, even unsympathetic recorder." [15] Certainly Elizabeth Peabody had a tremendous fear for her reputation; the following excerpts do not reflect the scrupulously honest recorder that she had previously claimed to be:

Elizabeth Peabody. Courtesy of the New York Public Library.

In the first place, in all these conversations where I have spoken, I should like to have that part of the conversation omitted, so that it may be felt that I was entirely passive. . . . I do not wish to appear as an interlocutor in the conversations either. Besides this, I must desire you to put a preface before mine, and express in it, in so many words, that on you rests all the responsibility of introducing the subjects and that your Recorder did not entirely sympathize or agree with you with respect to the course taken. . . .[16]

Boston reacted as Elizabeth Peabody had predicted. The city that was mobbing Irish Catholics and burning convents did not have much tolerance for Bronson Alcott's "heresy." The critics who had praised *Record of a School* now deplored the impropriety in Alcott's *Conversations:*

We cannot repress our indignation at the love of notoriety, for it can be nothing else, which will lead a man to scorn the truth and the best interests of society—and boldly defying public opinion and sentiments of the wise and good, to pollute the moral atmosphere, throw a stumbling block in the path of improvement. . . . Mr. Alcott should hide his head in shame.[17]

During all of this furor, Elizabeth Peabody had retreated to Salem. It was not until the last cries of indignation were silent that she again returned to Boston and attempted to open another school. Her behavior had been predictable; she chose to remain aloof from conflicts that might damage her reputation and force her to retreat from her activities. As an energetic, articulate woman she was vulnerable to numerous attacks, but none would be more serious than a questioning of her moral sensibilities—which involvement in Bronson Alcott's *Conversations* would surely have occasioned.

Peabody's avoidance of a confrontation only underscores her apparent fear. It was a fear not so much of conflict itself but of her perception of conflict and its implications. It is clear from the Temple School incident that she dreaded the defacement of her intensely moral image. That the ultimate responsibility of a teacher was to instill morality in children was her most cherished educational precept. And it was also a belief that many nineteenth-century Americans were beginning to associate especially with a woman's sphere: women, because of a supposedly innate moral sense, were particularly qualified to educate the young. This connection between women and morality was a crucial aspect of domesticity and really insured the survival of the ideology. Peabody well

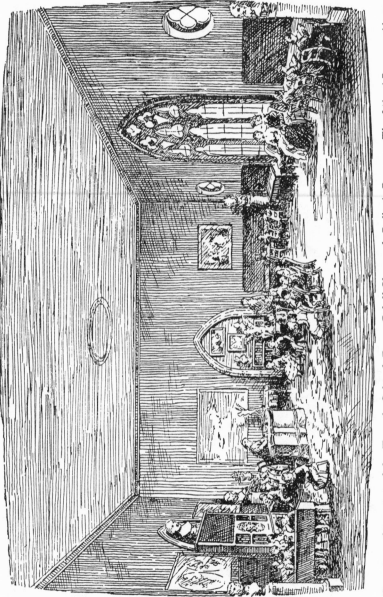

Drawing of interior of the Temple School. From Odell Shepard, *Pedlar's Progress: The Life of Bronson Alcott* (Boston: Little, Brown and Co., 1937).

understood this connection; although she did not often speak of *women's* unique moral aptitude, she did speak constantly about the primacy of morality as an educational goal. Indeed, this preoccupation with morality was her most direct tie with domestic ideals, for it is the only aspect of domesticity that she verbally and consciously promoted. If she were to be implicated in the Temple School scandal, she would not only be considered amoral, she would also be estranged from the domestic role in the eyes of Boston society. It was this separation that she tried so hard to avoid. Her passivity in the face of conflict shielded her from such an indictment.

Avoidance of this separation was not her only means of dealing with expected proper female behavior. Throughout her life she surrounded the relationships that she established as well as her institutional attachments with familial connotations. She sought a familial relationship with her associates. Her ability to involve herself in others' private lives was, perhaps, a natural extension of her conception of the woman as moral guardian. And since Elizabeth Peabody never married, her "family" came to include all who were open to her benevolent interference.

Often Peabody attached herself to people, particularly men, whose ideas she thought worthy of promotion. And most often Elizabeth Peabody placed herself in a motherly role. Her rather assertive yet sympathetic demeanor made the role seem entirely natural. Frequently, her more intense relationships were initiated when the object of her devotion was in a particularly weak state and in need of moral guidance. Thus, for example, she pushed Nathaniel Hawthorne—who eventually married her youngest sister, Sophia—out of unhappy seclusion into the limelight of Boston's literary circle.

Her relationship with Horace Mann, who also married one of her sisters, is particularly illustrative of her doting motherly disposition. Mr. Mann met Elizabeth Peabody and her sister Mary at Mrs. Clarke's boarding house in Boston, where he had come to recover from the death of his wife. Before too long, Elizabeth Peabody and Mr. Mann had long emotion-filled sessions, during which Elizabeth felt that it was her moral responsibility to help him in his time of misery. She wrote to her sister Sophia:

For my own part—my mind is torn between the desire that he may die as *he* wants to do—and my interest in that general good of society. . . . He looked up so gratefully—and yet so fondly—that it went to my very heart—and he still held my hand till Mary had gone

out of the room and then drew me nearer and throwing his arm
round me—let the tears flow—which ever seem to wait the touch of
sympathy.[18]

Surely Elizabeth Peabody was entirely content with this role of
comforter. Mann and Peabody sat for hours together in her private
parlor when Mann was bereaved. Gradually, though, they began to
speak more dispassionately about morality and religion, and Peabody
introduced Mann to such influential friends as Dr. William Ellery
Channing. Interestingly, Mann's friendship with Elizabeth abated and
his friendship with her less overbearing sister blossomed as his need for
heartrending sessions passed.

It was typical of Peabody to conduct her meetings in her "private
parlor." She often made her home the focus of her activities—whether
writing, teaching, meeting friends, or even running a business. Regardless of its use, the home remained a buffer, since it could shield her more
ambitious projects. In the early 1840s Elizabeth Peabody opened the
West Street Bookshop, which soon became the center for young
intellectuals, most of whom embraced the transcendental faith. It became
the meeting place where "newly born thoughts were received and
fostered." [19] It was there that

> whenever one looked in of a fine morning or afternoon, he met, as
> the chance might give, Mr. Allston the artist, Mr. Emerson, Mr.
> Ripley, Mr. Hawthorne, Mr. Hedge, not then doctor, Mr. Mann, or
> the Misses Peabody. . . . To one who remembers how very "En-
> glish" the training of young Boston had been till now—fed on
> Blackwood's, Frager's, the English quarterlies, it will seem that the
> opening of this modest reading room for books printed in France
> and Germany with a chance to meet those who read them most was
> an enlargement of the means of education.[20]

The bookshop, which specialized in books and periodicals that could not
be found elsewhere in Boston, also doubled as the Peabody home.
Elizabeth Peabody moved her family to West Street as soon as she
decided to open the store; they lived in the house, reserving the front
room of the lower story for the shop. But the shop was not really a
separation from the homelike intimacy of the rest of the Peabody
residence. In the front window of the "bookroom"—as the shop was
generally called—was a comfortable-looking rocker. Upon entering,
customers would be received as guests. They might browse through the
shelves which looked like bookcases in a rather large private library and

then, finding an appealing book, they might sit in a comfortable chair in the parlor-like room.[21]

Once the bookroom was running smoothly, Peabody expanded her activities and began to publish selected works. She undertook the publication of the *Dial* in the second year of its existence, and, when it folded, put out *Aesthetic Papers*, which included essays by Emerson, Hawthorne, and Thoreau as well as her own piece. Peabody's *Aesthetic Papers*, in addition to her own published articles and books, was received and praised by a small circle of Boston's intelligentsia. These intellectual endeavors, for Elizabeth Peabody, always had a moral purpose: "I never thought of any intellectual acquisition nor of any artistic power except as subservient to moral and social ends." [22] She never envisioned herself writing purely scholarly works. Rather—consistent with her feelings about the prominence of moral education and the qualifications of women in this area—she wrote pieces that probed past cultures in order to find models for her world. Her *Dorian Measure*, which was published in *Aesthetic Papers*, called attention to the early Greek commitment to the artistic, through which they symbolically expressed the order and harmony of the universe. Their education stressed the development of the mind as well as the body. Music, dance, and drawing were important aspects of a child's training; concentration on the aesthetic furthered both moral and intellectual development. Peabody decried the lack of these elements in the education of her day [23] and urged educators to learn from this early civilization.[24]

Margaret Fuller used Miss Peabody's bookroom to give her famous conversations to young women interested in literature and the fine arts. But Fuller never really approved of Elizabeth Peabody, whose "suffocating friendships made her repulsive." [25] Margaret Fuller, recoiling from Peabody's intense relationships, wrote: "Yet your tendency to extremes, as to personal attachments, is so strong, I am afraid you will not wholly rise above it. . . . The persons whom you have idolized can never, in the end, be ungrateful, and probably, at the time of retreat they still do justice to your heart. But, so long as you must draw persons too near you, a temporary recoil is sure to follow." [26]

Fuller's criticism of Peabody is indicative of more fundamental contrasts between the two women. Their differing feelings about femininity and domestic values insured that their styles would be antithetical. Fuller's ideal woman was a free spirit; her intellect, which always assumed a primacy for Fuller, would be unleashed, making her return to a state where neither intellectual—nor sexual or familial—straits were upon her. Released from convention, the woman "could recover her relationship to the sacred central energy from which her obligations sprang." [27] Fuller immersed herself in transcendental ideology, using it to free herself from traditional constraints upon her sex. In her writings and teaching she urged other women to allow free communication with their inner spirits and warned that the bleakness of family life would guarantee their servitude.

Fuller and Peabody associated with many of the same people, and, of course, had considerable association themselves. Although there was some mutual regard, Fuller had little patience with Peabody's apparent unconcern about issues "hostile to the character of woman." The word unconcern, however, is misleading. Peabody's unwillingness to confront questions about women's roles was due not to unconcern but to her own need to negotiate her numerous activities within the bounds of domestic proprieties. The contrast between the two women was stark: Fuller unleashed her energies untamed; Peabody carefully *managed* her life to avoid estranging herself from domesticity. Fuller would strive for individual liberation often without moral or societal constraints; Peabody would subserve all to social and particularly moral considerations. Indeed, she justified all of her activities in a moral context. It was in the realm of morality that her own justifications and the domestic ideology were most closely aligned.

Fuller's response to domesticity was not a common one for nineteenth-century women. Peabody, however, was more typical in that many women were faced with the problem of reconciling an increasingly pervasive domestic ideology with a desire for a more varied life. Peabody's reaction, which influenced the next generation's responses, helps to define the limits of change.

NOTES

1. Thomas Wentworth Higginson, "Pre-Collegiate Women," *Harper's Bazaar* (January 27, 1894): 62–63.

2. Elizabeth Palmer Peabody, "Female Education in Massachusetts: Reminiscences of Subjects and Methods of Teaching," *American Journal of Education* (July 1884): 307.

3. Ibid., p. 290.

4. Quoted in Odell Shepard, *Pedlar's Progress: The Life of Bronson Alcott* (Boston, 1937), p. 128 (see Note 15).

5. Percy Lubbock, *The Letters of Henry James* (New York, 1920), p. 116.

6. Ibid., p. 117.

7. Peabody, "Female Education in Massachusetts," p. 309.

8. Ibid. Miss Peabody became more aware of the feminist struggle late in her life. She later admitted that the women's movement was an inevitable protest against the degraders of women. But this acknowledgment did not come until

well after the Civil War. Perhaps by then the struggle had become more respectable, and her reputation more firmly entrenched.

9. Josephine E. Roberts, "Elizabeth Peabody and the Temple School," *The New England Quarterly* 15 (September 1942): 499 (see Note 15).

10. Quoted in Shepard, p. 129.

11. Elizabeth Palmer Peabody, *Record of a School: Exemplifying the Great Principles of Spiritual Culture* (Boston, 1835), pp. 157–58.

12. Review in *Christian Examiner and General Review* 19 (November 1835): 270.

13. Bronson Alcott, *Conversations on the Gospels,* quoted in Shepard, p. 186.

14. Letter from Elizabeth Peabody to Mary Peabody, week of April 11, 1936, *Cuba Journal,* Berg Collection, New York Public Library. The *Cuba Journal* consists of letters written by Elizabeth and her two sisters when the latter were in Cuba, where Sophia was recovering from an illness.

15. Dorothy McCluskey, *Bronson Alcott, Teacher* (New York, 1940), pp. 99–100. Secondary source material discussing the Temple School crisis widely varies in interpretation of the incident. The interpretations are uniformly partisan, either in favor of Alcott or Peabody. None of the sources reveals the complexity of the incident—particularly with respect to Peabody's ambivalencies.

McCluskey depicts Peabody as a woman whose "constancy" failed her and who "scurried and crawled to escape" (p. 99). Similarly, Odell Sheppard, also Alcott's biographer, accuses Peabody of duplicity. Neither volume attempts to analyze Peabody's predicament. Josephine Roberts in her article in the *New England Quarterly*—written after the publication of these two books—attempts to discount "printed sources" which gave a false impression of Peabody's role. But Roberts, in trying to vindicate Peabody, depicts Peabody as a virtual heroine. While ignoring the severity of the conflict as well as the possible reasons for Peabody's behavior, Roberts focuses upon Peabody's role as "first promoter, chief recorder, and last defender of Alcott's Temple School" (p. 508).

16. Letter from Elizabeth Peabody to Bronson Alcott from Worcester, August 7, 1836, quoted in Shepard, pp. 187–89.

17. Article by "A Parent" in *Boston Courier,* quoted in Shepard, p. 193.

18. E. P. P. to Sophia, no date, Berg Collection.

19. Van Wyck Brooks, *The Flowering of New England* (New York, 1936), p. 238.

20. James Freeman Clarke, *Autobiography, Diary and Correspondence,* ed. Edward Hale (Boston, 1891), p. 143.

21. Louise Hall Tharp, *The Peabody Sisters of Salem* (Boston, 1937), p. 28. Tharp's gossipy biography provides—along with its oversimplifications and sugar-coated portraits—some picturesque details, about the bookshop, for example.

22. Peabody, "Female Education in Massachusetts," p. 307.

23. In Froebel, Elizabeth Peabody eventually found an educational philosophy that championed the use of the aesthetic. He worked out a series of artistic exercises to draw forth the powers of children from a profound depth.

24. Elizabeth P. Peabody, "The Dorian Measure," in *Aesthetic Papers,* ed. Elizabeth Peabody (Boston, 1849), pp. 64–110.

25. Barbara Cross, *The Educated Woman in America* (New York, 1965), p. 22.

Cross's volume, which combines cogently written interpretive essays with excerpts from primary source selections, is the only attempt to discuss educated women of different time periods with a view to comparison. Cross does draw some interesting contrasts between Catharine Beecher, Margaret Fuller, and Martha Carey Thomas, and primary source material is often very suggestive as well. She does not, though, attempt to apply a theoretical framework for discussing these women so that one might know whether differences and similarities are accidental or a function of time and place.

26. Quoted in Cross, p. 129.

27. Ibid., p. 19.

CHAPTER I

Alice Freeman Palmer:
Power, Domesticity, and Wellesley College

Alice Freeman Palmer belonged to a generation where girls with intellectual promise occasionally persuaded their reluctant parents to send them to college. Informal aggregations such as Margaret Fuller's conversations were largely replaced by formal institutions; women who had previously paid twenty-five dollars to hear Fuller's "oral lectures" or who had spent hours alone reading Plato might now attend a college where their intellectual development would be carefully programmed. The emergence of self-educated nineteenth-century women helped to highlight the need for institutions that would bring intellectually gifted women into close rapport.

Once in college, women not only faced a formal intellectual program but also had to confront ideas about proper spheres for women. Leaders of colleges differed as to suitable roles, but all had ideals that they attempted to inculcate. The close association of women in colleges made the seeming indifference of an Elizabeth Peabody to questions about acceptable womanly occupations virtually impossible. In addition, women's colleges insured visibility for their students, as family, friends, and curious onlookers waited to see if they would turn into suffragettes or model wives and mothers. Thus, it would have been difficult for early college women to remain inarticulate about either their own aspirations or their views concerning women's roles. Some, of course, were more inclined to confront such subjects than others, but none could easily be as elusive as Elizabeth Peabody.

Alice Palmer attended the University of Michigan from 1872 to 1876. She went to Michigan because in 1872 women's colleges had not yet attained the stature of the coeducational institutions.[1] Requirements were not as difficult in women's colleges, and courses of study included college preparatory work as well as more regular study.[2] After several years of teaching in both private schools and at Wellesley College, Alice Freeman Palmer became Wellesley's president. As a college woman and as the head of a college, it was certainly incumbent upon her to discuss her ideas of worthy ambitions for educated women. She made many pronouncements on the subject, both in speeches and writings, and all testify to a basic relief that a woman's most sacred role was as wife and mother. But she believed that these roles could be expanded so that women—particularly educated women—might reach the young and infirm in the larger society as well as in the home. Thus she encouraged women whose home responsibilities were not too overwhelming to pursue careers in teaching and philanthropic work. Her notions of careers in this latter field were very vague; it was up to the next generation of college women to define more precisely charitable careers suitable for women. Yet despite some lack of definition, Alice Freeman Palmer, unlike Elizabeth Peabody, had begun to talk directly about acceptable spheres of feminine concern.

Many of Alice Palmer's thoughts on the subject of women seem to have been influenced by her mother who, like Elizabeth Peabody's mother, was a strong force in her family and helped to support her husband and children by teaching. Mrs. Freeman believed in the sanctity of the home and family and viewed teaching young children as the logical extension of the moral woman's responsibilities. She was, in addition, committed to certain reformist causes and spent much of her time crusading for temperance.[3] When Alice Freeman wished to go to college, her mother, despite her own active life, was extremely reluctant, thinking that a college education was inappropriate for a young woman whose activities should never lead her too far from the hearthside. Alice Freeman persuaded both parents, however, promising that she would try to put her brother through college and see that her two younger sisters received whatever education they wished.[4]

Palmer's activities did in fact take her far from the hearthside. Yet the family was, for her, always the primary point of reference and of attachment, despite her wanderings from the home. It was always difficult for her to reconcile rigorous intellectual training for women with her feelings about the primacy of the family, and much of her energies at Wellesley were consumed in trying to mold college women whose intellect and womanliness would be combined so as to insure their superior ability to pursue roles as wives, mothers, teachers, and charity workers. The intellect would subserve and preserve domesticity in all of its variations. But these formulas did not really apply to Alice Freeman Palmer's own life. As president of Wellesley College she had amassed power and influence; her prominence within a rather large institutional structure did not fit images of submissive wives and mothers whose arena was limited to homes, schools for young children, and churches. Executive ability was decidedly unfeminine, and Alice Freeman Palmer was widely known for possessing this quality.

Thus she faced the same problem that Elizabeth Peabody had encountered a generation before: how to reconcile a fundamental belief in the sacredness of the wife and mother role with her own departure from that image. Being a public figure, Alice Freeman Palmer could not ignore the conflict. She attempted to resolve it by seeing herself as part of a family and constantly describing her situation using familial metaphors. Alice Palmer tried both to pay homage to domesticity and to convey a personal image that was consistent with her pronouncements.[5] Elizabeth Peabody never really articulated either the problem or her solution; her intimate relationships were obviously of a familial character and her constant movement from one relationship to another and from one institution to another couched her conflict.

At Wellesley, Alice Freeman spoke of herself as head of a large family. She knew all Wellesley women, whom she referred to as "my girls," by their first names, tried to remember details about each girl, and encouraged them to visit her office which—reminiscent of Elizabeth Peabody—was described by a member of the faculty as a "private parlor."[6] She tried to combine power and responsibility with familial serenity, and attempted to create an atmosphere of homelike intimacy within a publicly scrutinized institution. This situation might have remained stable for Alice Freeman had she not met George Herbert Palmer; his marriage proposal destroyed the reconciliation that she had achieved and forced her both to face the reality of her power at Wellesley and to reckon with her feelings and pronouncements about the sanctity of marriage. Moreover, Palmer's responses to her dilemma help to point to the nature of the attacks upon educated women who ventured from the hearthside into the public world reserved for men.

Alice Freeman met George Herbert Palmer in 1884. She was the dynamic young president of Wellesley and he was Harvard's moral philosopher. At first they saw each other only occasionally at academic functions in Boston. But by 1886 they were corresponding regularly, and the relationship grew more serious. In the middle of that year, Professor Palmer was urging her to leave Wellesley College and marry him.

From the beginning, Palmer never entertained the possibility that some compromise might be reached, that each of them might be able to retain their respective positions and still maintain a married life together. When Alice Freeman timidly raised the possibility of his coming to Wellesley, Palmer reacted strongly: "I am sure you would feel it somewhat humiliating to see me marry into a position." [7] But obviously it was Palmer who would have felt the humiliation, as his letters testify to an underlying current of intense resentment of her position and competitive jealousy. When she wrote him excitedly of a proposed honorary degree that she would be receiving at Columbia University, he answered: "I can't match your honors, but did I tell you that a month ago the Academy of Arts and Sciences asked me to become a member and that I declined?" [8] By making light of such honorary awards, his comment undermines the significance of her honor.

Professor Palmer basically disapproved of Alice Freeman's position at Wellesley, and his disapproval went beyond personal indignation. His letters reveal that he saw no connection whatever between femininity and an active career. To him, her power and influence were incompatible with womanliness, and her attempts at creating a familial atmosphere were a sham. Wellesley College could never provide a real home atmosphere for her: it was impossible to combine the privacy that a woman should have with a public position. He wrote: "Your private life will tend more and more to shrivel . . . while your public life goes its way more and more as a matter of business." [9]

The woman belonged at home. There her private life would assume the importance that it should. There, too, she could pursue "worthy" activities. But these—never clearly defined—would emanate from a secure, warm home life; they could never assume primacy. It was in the home that she would be a "true woman." George Palmer often characterized this "true woman" as a dependent "little girl" [10] who would not quell his need—openly acknowledged in his letters—to domineer. Thus, the ideal woman was portrayed by Palmer—as by many other nineteenth-century Americans—as submissive and childlike.

This delicate creature would need to be cared for in the confines of a home. Palmer constantly admonished Freeman about the effect of so much pressured activity on her health, echoing a favorite theme of opponents of women's higher education. He harped on it constantly; indeed, his campaign was so successful that, when Alice Freeman finally did resign, she announced that a prime reason for her leaving was her failing health. Implicit in his statements was the idea that the fragility of women made such a frenzied life as she led absurd—or, as he put it, suicidal: "I worship a glorious *woman* in you, and believe that she is the one you were meant to be. . . . You think they are sacrifices which you are justified in making to a great institution. To me they look like suicide." [11]

It was from a home base, maintained George Palmer, that "you will be stronger . . . for yourself, for every good purpose for which the Lord made you, than you can possibly by continuing longer a public functionary." [12] Believing that the Lord certainly did not make women to become college presidents, Palmer emphasized his feelings by denigrating her position in an extremely harsh manner. In his letters he would never attach any real importance to her work at Wellesley, preferring instead to attack her motives and ambitions which, he contended, were ruining her health as well as her femininity. Her accumulation of power was most repugnant to him, and in an almost mocking tone he wrote: "Formerly you were a princess here. Everyone obeyed you and you looked up to no one. Has someone broken in or stolen your crown and made a common person out of you, one like the rest of the world, so that you are likely now to lose a kingdom and authority and even your power of largess?" [13]

Reading this statement, one might imagine Freeman to be insatiably ambitious, even guileful in her desire to rule. In his impatience to have her leave Wellesley, Professor Palmer was emphasizing that aspect of her life that he disliked most vehemently and even feared; he also knew, of course, that she would be repelled by such an image of herself—that its incongruity with sweet, submissive femininity had caused her to be extremely careful to avoid such indictments.

His arguments proved too overwhelming for Alice Freeman, who found herself becoming increasingly unsure about her commitment to Wellesley. Unable any longer to ignore the ambivalence that she felt toward her work, she began to dichotomize future possibilities in an exaggerated manner. Her feelings began to approach those of Palmer. She characterized marriage as a life of warm, personal contact tinged with docility and sacrifice and pictured staying at Wellesley as pursuing a life filled solely with dedication to duty. She would, particularly in the beginning of their correspondence, often dismiss thoughts of marriage, calling it impossible. On one occasion she wrote: "But I trust you perfectly to need no argument in behalf of the convictions of duty, whether you agree with them or not." [14]

Gradually, she began to reveal a certain impatience with life at Wellesley and viewed the domestic touches of college life with boredom and a tinge of condescension. For example, on one occasion, the girls had arranged an "at home" with music. She wrote: "When they unfolded their pretty plan tonite, I found my imagination unequal to the situation." [15] It is significant that these domesticlike joys of college life, which had been the source of her reconciliation of the conflict between womanliness and her career, no longer provided any satisfaction.

Increasingly, she saw satisfaction in marrying George Herbert Palmer. She acknowledged a growing need to be docile in her letters, and seemed to enjoy George Palmer's references to her as his "little girl." His attempt to lay bare her power at Wellesley was very effective, for she now would retreat from the harsh public glare and proclaim the spiritual joys of domesticity without feeling that her own life wavered from such a sacred path. In one of her published poems she wrote:

> Great love has triumphed. At a crisis hour
> Of strength and struggle on the heights of life
> He came, and bidding me abandon power
> Called me to take the quiet name of wife.[16]

She left the college in December of 1887. And although life with George Herbert Palmer was never really "quiet," since she worked diligently on many charitable causes, she never again attained the power and influence that her years as Wellesley's president had brought her. Leaving Wellesley symbolized, to both of them, the end of her individuality and the beginning of her dependency and merged identity. Professor Palmer wrote: "This is the last love letter I shall ever write you—at least while you are still you." [17] In a poem entitled "Surrender," composed soon after she was married, Alice Freeman Palmer wrote:

> For my heart is in Spring
> And he is its sun
> He is lord of my world,
> And new life has begun.
> Take the sceptre my king!
> All I am you have won.[18]

The pattern of Palmer's life provides a contrast to that of Elizabeth Peabody's, and, consequently, points to changes in the concept of domesticity. Boston society in the 1830s and 1840s permitted Peabody to attend to her activities, all of which were justified by moral considerations. She carefully arranged her homelike settings, but these settings were all fairly ephemeral. Her movement was largely unhampered, making her inclinations—whether to start a school or to open a bookshop—appear natural and unrestrained. She managed not to stray too far from the "home" by having her various homes serve different purposes. The impression she gave, despite her careful attempt to connect herself with the "home" and familial relationships, was of a natural emoting of morality within a society that accepted her behavior.

Palmer, though, had a far more explicit set of domestic values to contend with. The code of feminine duty, although still very much based upon the view of women as moral and regenerative forces, was now tied more definitely to particular settings. One's own home and family was the central focus. In the late 1840s and 1850s especially, there was an immense proliferation of manuals, domestic novels, and articles in women's magazines which tried to guide women on proper methods for rearing their children, cleaning their houses, and caring for the spiritual needs of their families. The cumulative effect was to confine women more completely, spatially now as well as ideologically. (Even women schoolteachers in Palmer's generation were less enterprising than their mothers, for they usually taught in established schools rather than starting their own.) This confinement to particular tasks in particular places led to a strengthened notion that women were the supported class. When a woman married—or "surrendered"—her sphere was defined for her. George Palmer's inability to accept Alice Freeman's role as Wellesley's president is clearly related to the concept of women as a supported class. He needed her to be financially as well as emotionally dependent upon him. Furthermore, the competitive feelings that he had about her particular brand of work contributed to the intensity of his opposition to her continuing as president. Indeed, it becomes more and more apparent throughout the nineteenth century that many academic men—in both coeducational and male institutions—feared an overlapping of the roles of educated men and women. In colleges men and women could compete for academic honors; yet this competition could not be continued after graduation. Spheres had to be kept separate. And university men throughout the century seemed intent not only on providing "scientific" evidence of innate differences [19] but also on supporting separate courses of study. Their turf was being encroached upon, and the invasion needed to be kept under control.

Alice Freeman Palmer's involvement with questions of domesticity—as opposed to Elizabeth Peabody's apparent indifference to them—is not, then, due only to the former's visibility as president of Wellesley College. The aspects of domestic ideology had become more particularized and explicit and thus far more difficult to ignore by 1880. For Palmer, the female college, divorced at least physically from the source of opposition to women's independence, became a place where she could try, without bending the framework of domesticity too significantly, to work out a way for intelligent women to add some depth to a life of household chores. It became a place where women might learn to blend the intellect with the domestic, thus becoming more active managers of their own lives.

NOTES

1. See George Herbert Palmer, *The Life of Alice Freeman Palmer* (Boston, 1910), for the best description of her early life. Palmer's biography of his wife is a sentimental account and reveals his strong biases toward her "sweet womanliness." It does, however, contain some information not found elsewhere about details of her life and also contains excerpts from her letters.

2. For a comparison of course requirements see Woody, vol. 2.

3. Again, for details of Palmer's early life see George Herbert Palmer's biography. This information is on p. 17.

4. Ibid., p. 42.

5. See William Taylor, *Cavalier & Yankee: The Old South and American National Character* (New York, 1961) for a discussion of Sarah Hale, whose *Godey's Lady's Book* more than any other single source helped to carve a domestic sphere for American women. Taylor discusses (pp. 120-21) this same double role dilemma with respect to Hale who, on the one hand, eulogized the woman's place in the family and, on the other hand, became a shrewd businesswoman. Taylor writes: "If this involved her in inconsistencies, she could at least have argued she had never recommended the role to anyone else" (p. 121).

6. Florence Converse, *The Story of Wellesley* (Boston, 1915), comment by Professor Whiting on p. 72. Converse's history of Wellesley is typical of the bulk of college histories, which essentially use as their theme the unfolding of an important institution. Particular college histories, like this one, most often do not place the institution in a larger context. The most valuable information they contain are bits of personal letters, quotations like this one, and, in some cases— although not in this one—a list of sources. Also, one gains a sense of chronology from Converse.

7. *An Academic Courtship—Letters of Alice Freeman and George Herbert Palmer 1886-1887* (Cambridge, Mass., 1940), George to Alice, April 1887. This fascinating group of letters is very revealing of the intensity of the conflict between Alice Freeman and George Herbert Palmer. Caroline Hazard, a later president of Wellesley and an admirer of Alice Palmer, wrote the Introduction, in which she acknowledged that the letters tell of an "internal struggle" (p. xxvi). It is interesting that, despite the publication of this volume, a very recent account of Palmer's life by Barbara Solomon in *Notable American Women*, ed. Edward T. James, vol. 2 (Cambridge, Mass., 1971), does not acknowledge that a "struggle" existed: "Alice Freeman Palmer understood what she had given up in marrying and had no conflict about her decision."

8. Ibid., G to A, January 1887.

9. Ibid., G to A, December 3, 1886.

10. This phrase was used constantly by George Herbert Palmer in his letters.

11. Ibid., G to A, December 3, 1886.

12. Ibid., G to A, July 1886.

13. Ibid., G to A, August 30, 1886.

14. Ibid., A to G, July 1886.

15. Ibid., A to G, September 27, 1886.

16. Alice Freeman Palmer, *A Marriage Cycle* (Boston, 1915), poem entitled "Retrospect." This collection of poems shows the extent to which she—in George Palmer's words—"profoundly honored marriage." It is interesting that George Palmer decided that they were not too intimate to print despite her wish that they be burned after her death. The poems reveal the side of her that he, of course, felt most comfortable with and wished to share with the world.

17. *An Academic Courtship*, G to A, December 1887.

18. Palmer, *A Marriage Cycle.*

19. Aside from the more widely quoted books on the subject such as G. Stanley Hall's *Adolescence* (New York, 1904) and Edward Clarke's *Sex in Education, or a Fair Chance for the Girls* (Boston, 1873), there were numerous articles on the subject, particularly in the *Journal of Heredity* and in the *Popular Science Monthly.*

CHAPTER II

Martha Carey Thomas: The Scholarly Ideal and the Bryn Mawr Woman

When in 1899 Martha Carey Thomas, the young and spirited president of Bryn Mawr College, accused the venerated president of Harvard University, Charles Eliot, of having "sun spots" on his brain, the account was carried in newspapers across the country. Her presumption was a rarity among even educated women whose preoccupation with conflicts between womanliness and intellect often necessitated withdrawal from issues that would bring the ambiguity to the surface. But Martha Carey Thomas took a firm stand in favor of the intellect, and her fierce rhetoric attests to her willingness—even eagerness—to confront those who argued that the feminine nature stood in opposition to rigorous intellectual training.

In pitting herself against Charles Eliot, Thomas confronted the anti-feminist argument in highly articulate, well-reasoned form. In his early speeches and writings, Eliot had claimed that women had neither the intelligence nor the need to study the great traditions of learning inherited from the past. Although he eventually changed his mind about women's innate abilities, he never wavered from the conviction that different groups served separate and distinct functions and should be educated accordingly. He was "vividly aware of the importance Darwinism attached to individual variation," [1] and believed that the natural and fitting duties of groups would complement each other. Eliot claimed that the value of an occupation was to be judged by its product, and that the result of these normal or natural duties would contribute to the progress of the human race—progress toward public justice and happiness, the chief ends of mankind.[2]

The natural duties of women consisted, according to Eliot, in making family life more productive; the products of a serviceable woman's care—dutiful, thoughtful, loving children—would confirm the great importance of her natural occupation for the progress of humanity. Eliot wrote that "the prime motive of the higher education of women should be recognized as the development in women of the capacities and powers which will fit them to make family life and social life more intelligent, more enjoyable, happier, and more productive—more productive in every sense, physically, mentally, and spiritually."[3]

It was inevitable, perhaps, said Eliot, that ambitious women leaders should have tried to direct the higher education of women toward bringing them into new occupations, particularly into the professions as men have made them. "But wiser ways and methods will come into play, because it is not the chief happiness or the chief end of women, as a whole, to enter these new occupations, or to pursue them through life. They enter many which they soon abandon, and that is well—particularly the abandonment!"[4] Certainly, Eliot considered Thomas to be one of those ambitious leaders who, in her desire to bring women into new professions, was undermining public justice and happiness.

Carey Thomas never answered Eliot's contentions in a systematic, logical fashion. Rather, her rhetoric was often rambling and too "energetically unreflective"[5] to be always consistent and concise. In her zeal to provide educated women with sufficient armor to combat stultifying domestic lives, she spoke with forceful metaphors. Her responses to Eliot were not meted out on a philosophical plane; rather, she attacked and confronted on a very personal level while picking out those points that she could, with her dramatic images, attempt to reduce to absurdity. Thus, after Eliot had given a speech welcoming a new president of Wellesley College in which he said that liberal arts curricula of women's colleges were too imitative of those of men's colleges, President Thomas used her opening address at Bryn Mawr College in 1899 to reply:

As progressive as one may be in education or in other things there may be in our minds some dark spot of mediaevalism, and clearly in President Eliot's otherwise luminous intelligence women's education is this dark spot. He might as well have told the president of Wellesley to invent a new Christian religion for Wellesley or new

symphonies and operas, a new Beethoven and Wagner, new statues
and pictures, a new Phidias and a new Titian, new tennis, new golf,
a new way to swim, skate and run, new food, and new drink. It
would be easier to do all this than to create for women a new
science of geography, a new Greek Tragedies, new chemistry, new
philosophies, in short a new intellectual heavens and earth.[6]

Eliot's opinions on women were derived from a view of the world that
disavowed uniformity of group functions. Carey Thomas, however, did
not operate from a comprehensive image of the world. Her arena was
much less encompassing, and it consisted primarily of well-educated
men and women. But for her, these groups were not to function as static
units performing complementary, unchanging functions whose value
would be judged by their products. Instead of complementary functions
she envisioned the struggle for superiority. The process of this competition and not the product of "natural" occupations was, for Thomas, the
basic component of progress. If Eliot employed Darwinian theory to
justify the status quo for women, Carey Thomas used his notion of
competition and struggle to urge women out of the home and into the
"battlefield": "in the higher grade, that is in college teaching, women are
just beginning to compete with men, and this competition is beset with
the bitterest professional jealousy that women have ever had to meet,
except perhaps in medicine. . . . Women have succeeded so brilliantly,
on the whole so much better than men, as primary and secondary
teachers, that they will undoubtedly repeat this success in their college
teaching as soon as artificial restrictions are removed." [7]

It is clear that Martha Carey Thomas did not, at least early in her life,
make concessions to domesticity as Alice Palmer and Elizabeth Peabody
did. Her disagreements with Eliot were indicative of her rejection of the
woman's role as submissive and passive even if her servility would be
extended to those who needed her outside of the home. Thomas wished
to prove women's equal—if not superior—abilities, and, in order to do
this, men and women had to compete in the same arenas. It was in the
area of academics and research that Carey Thomas believed women
would best be able to demonstrate their strength.

Her choice of scholarship as a proving ground for women—with its
concomitant elements of graduate work and university teaching [8]—
stemmed, in part, from what she referred to as a natural disposition that
had its origins in her childhood. She spoke of her younger years as
preparation for these "higher pursuits" in the same passionate, effusive
language with which she chided her critics; the almost unidimensional
way in which she pictured her early life as paving the way for her later

interests is evidence that image making was very important to her. It is clearly true, though, that she had a rebellious nature and that she was resentful of limitations placed upon her because of her sex and beliefs about women's intellectual inferiority. She wrote of begging God to kill her if it were indeed true that she could never master Greek and go to college. She claimed to have wept over the account of Adam and Eve, fearing that Eve's curse might imperil girls' attending college. She wrote:

> I can well remember one endless scorching summer's day when sitting in a hammock under the trees with a French dictionary, blinded by tears more burning than the July sun, I translated the most indecent book I have ever read, Michelet's famous—were it not now forgotten, I should say infamous—book on women, *La femme*. I was beside myself with terror lest it might prove true that I myself was so vile and pathological a thing.[9]

Despite the difficulty in sorting exaggerations from reality in Thomas's writing, it is evident that she did attach a special significance to scholarly pursuits early in her life. She seemed to see scholarship as serious and significant enough to be an antidote to women's frivolity, which she claimed to witness in her own family. Thomas's parents were prominent Quakers who consistently indulged Martha, their oldest child, born in 1857. She had always been "bent on pre-eminence, and she resented the privileges granted her four younger brothers, her father, and the masculine sex in general." [10] Yet her father was a doctor and a scholar, and it was his life rather than that of her mother that she sought to emulate. Her mother's preoccupations with upper-class parties and philanthropies bored and even appalled her: "I ain't going to get married and I don't want to teach school. I can't imagine anything worse than living a regular young lady's life. . . . I don't care if everybody would cut me." [11] Martha Carey Thomas pictured her mother's life as wasteful, and she saw no way of coming to terms with "the frivolities of a society girl and the servitude of the matron" [12] except by rejecting the whole way of life.

The choice of academia as the vehicle for escape was not unprecedented for women who had never achieved prominence in other fields reserved for men such as law, medicine, or finance. There were notable women intellects both in Europe and America whose notoriety was perhaps more visible to the surrounding societies than their intellectual achievements. The mocking eighteenth-century term "bluestocking," used to describe educated or literary women, testifies to their presence. Margaret Fuller, who a generation before had proclaimed her faith in the freed intelligence, was certainly a precursor. Yet the differences in the way Fuller and Thomas viewed the intellect are significant. Fuller had in the 1830s and 1840s proclaimed her faith in the emancipated intellect, not only as an end in itself but as a way of releasing women from domestic servitude. Her image was of mindless, bored matrons becoming attuned to their inner energies which longed to be released. Fuller's means of release was a process which, although containing similar elements for all women, was a highly individualized one. Self-education was the key, for she saw the traditional classical education as sterile and monotonous with its emphasis upon rote and rhetoric. It was this process—rather than any emerging society that might result from it—that was essential to Fuller. Fifty years later, Carey Thomas also saw the intellect as providing liberation for women. But the process—as well as the end result—was to be highly controlled. Higher education provided a vehicle for this discipline; institutional settings would tame the intellect. The "liberation" itself was restricted, for Thomas chose the particular areas that she wanted women to pursue. And, indeed, it was not individual liberation that mattered as much as the advancement of women in general and their ability to compete with men. Thomas insisted upon women's achievement, but she did not, as did Fuller, insist upon the companion ideas of initiative and individuality. Her agenda was not for the individual but for the group—and she believed that the female college would help her to carry through that agenda.

Thomas herself attended educational institutions. A college education was available in 1874, and Carey Thomas, unlike other upper-class girls, chose to go to college rather than to spend several years abroad acquiring a taste for Old World culture. Despite her family's interest in education, they resisted her attempts to attend college, for it was not considered the role of a socially prominent young lady to go to college. A college education was more suitable to daughters of upper-middle-class and middle-class families who could afford the tuition and who were not obeisant to high society's image of the woman who was cultivated yet decidedly not a bookworm.[13] Thomas was warned that a college education might scare away prospective husbands. "According to her cousin Logan Pearsall Smith, the Baltimore clan found her desire for a college education as shocking a choice as a life of prostitution."[14] However, she did go to Cornell in 1874.

She chose Cornell primarily for the same reason that Alice Freeman Palmer chose the University of Michigan: women's colleges were not yet academically respected and thus did not offer an alternative to established coeducational institutions. Thomas spurned Vassar as "an advanced female seminary."[15] Before going to Cornell, Thomas had herself attended a female seminary—the Howland Institute, a school near Ithaca, New York. It was founded and run by the Howland family who were Quakers and knew the Thomases. Thus, Carey Thomas's attendance at Cornell—a short distance from Howland and founded also by a Quaker, Ezra Cornell—was not surprising. Certainly, the interconnection of family and religious ties was comforting to families who were sending their daughters away to school.

At Cornell Thomas was disappointed by the "frivolity of the women students." [16] She must also have been disappointed by—or certainly keenly aware of—the Cornell tradition of "anticoedism." Her later associations with Cornell as a trustee and an eminent alumna made her an apologist for Cornell, and she did not dwell upon undergraduate experiences that might have been disturbing. Andrew D. White, president of the university from 1866 to 1885, favored coeducation, and in a defense of girls' attendance he wrote:

> Strong men, in adversity and perplexity, have often found that the "partners of their joys and sorrows" give no more real strength than would Nuremberg dolls. Under this theory, as thus worked out, the aid and counsel and solace fail just when they are most needed. In their stead the man is likely to find some scraps of philosophy begun in boarding-schools and developed in kitchens and drawing rooms.[17]

White's attitude toward women's learning was more enlightened than that of his fellow president, Charles Eliot, who had not yet even accepted any need for female higher education. Yet White's defense was less than radical: he would have women become intelligent and cultivated marriage partners, able to offer their husbands astute advice instead of "fetishisms and superstitions." Many of Cornell's students, though, plainly resented the presence of women. Whether from their feeling that women deflected any pretense of Ivy League status or from a general acceptance of a common belief that college was no place for women, the "cold-shouldering of the females by the males existed from the first" and continued at least until the First World War.[18] This reaction must surely have strengthened rather than diminished Thomas's competitiveness; it most likely, too, encouraged her belief that coeducation was a phenomenon that might only flourish in the future. Given the attitudes of resistance on the part of academic men, Thomas, even more directly than Palmer, saw the female college as a place where women's convictions and intellect might be strengthened without the interference of hostile forces.

But Thomas did not loiter at Cornell for "reconsiderations." With a fixity of purpose that left family and friends in awe of her, she left for the University of Leipzig to confront the rigors of a German university. She found the culture of Europe exhilarating, labored at philology, and dismissed the male students as dull.[19] But since Leipzig did not give the doctorate to women, Carey Thomas left for Zurich, and received the degree *summa cum laude* for her dissertation entitled "Sir Gawayne and the Green Knight." Interestingly, she found the study grueling and seemed to think of the many hours of research as boring and tedious. It becomes even more apparent from this personal experience that her interest was not in the scholarship itself but in the products or rewards of that scholarship, which would prove her triumph as a woman. When she talked to others about the joys of renouncing other preoccupations for the intellectual life—or, as she called it, "intellectual renunciation"—her words seem hollow, for it was the dignity of women and not the rigor of research that she was promoting.

Once at Bryn Mawr she hoped to prevent frivolity as she sought to fashion and perfect "the type of Bryn Mawr woman which will, we hope, become as well known and universally admired a type as the Oxford and Cambridge man or the graduate of the great English public schools." [20] Such a woman, she hoped, would be equipped to take up the gauntlet and enter a "gallant struggle" where "pitfalls lie on all sides of us; controversies past and present darken the air: our path leads us thru hard-won battlefields." [21] She would also be capable of enduring a life of intellectual renunciation. Her priorities were staunch:

> The highest service which colleges can render to their time is to discover and foster imaginative and constructive genius. Such genius unquestionably needs opportunity for its highest development. . . . Ability of the kind I am speaking of is, of course, very rare, but for this reason it is precious beyond all other human products. . . . It seems to me then to rest with us, the college women of this generation, to see to it that the girls of the next generation are given favorable conditions for this higher kind of scholarly development.[22]

During her first several decades at Bryn Mawr, Carey Thomas was intent on producing this mission-oriented woman whose sense of purpose would be strong enough to subdue feelings of loneliness and occasional discouragement. Knowing that other women were pursuing a scholarly life might also be of great comfort. "Sex solidarity," according to Thomas, was becoming a very compelling force in the world. She wrote: "As I watch their gallant struggles I sometimes think that the very stars in their courses are conspiring against them. Women scholars can assist women students, as men can not, to tide over the first discouragements of a life of intellectual renunciation." [23]

Ideas of competition between the sexes, lives of intellectual renunciation, and sex solidarity were, of course, inconsistent with the acceptance of marriage as an alternative—particularly for Carey Thomas's idealized scholars. In a widely quoted passage she strongly affirmed her belief that ambitious careers and marriage were diametrical opposites: "Women scholars have another and still more cruel handicap. They have spent half a lifetime in fitting themselves for their chosen work and then may be asked to choose between it and marriage. No one can estimate the number of women who remain unmarried in revolt before such a horrible alternative." [24] Carey Thomas herself, of course, remained unmarried. Her emphasis on sex solidarity coupled with occasional statements predicting women's natural but as yet unblossomed superiority—particularly in the areas of academics and college teaching—reveal a definite elitism and separatism in her thinking. She was an isolationist with respect to men, living most of her adult life with close women friends [25] surrounded by a college filled with women students.

She did realize, however, that not all women graduates—not even all of those from Bryn Mawr—would become Madame Curies or even outstanding scholars. She recognized and seemed to accept the inevitable fact that some women college graduates "will marry in a rather deliberate fashion." [26] She even publicly subscribed to the rather popular defense of women's higher education which rested on the premise that a college education increased the probability that both men and women would "live and work together as comrades and dear friends and married friends and lovers." [27] But she added a less popular qualifier: "their effectiveness and happiness and the welfare of the generation to come after them will be vastly increased if their college education has given them the same intellectual training and the same scholarly and moral ideas." [28] It was crucial, according to Thomas, that this education be the same for both sexes. She told those men who claimed that a woman's college education should make provisions for the wifely and motherly roles to "begin by educating their own college men to be husbands." [29]

Her abrupt retorts left no doubt that, despite statements sentimentalizing the love and respect between college men and women, the separatist strain in her thinking as well as her basic distrust of men's motives ran deep. She believed that an isolated women's institution would best be able to mold the woman whose mind would not be tainted by thoughts of sex, marriage, and children—all of which interfered with women's achievements: "It is undesirable to have the problems of love and marriage presented for decision to a young girl during the four years when she ought to devote her energies to profiting by the only systematic intellectual training she is likely to receive during her life." [30] She occasionally, however, deferred to the benefits of a coeducational institution, for at least, she said, it assured women of equal educational opportunity which some of the more compromising institutions for women did not supply. Also, coeducation might provide the ambitious woman with "the priceless associations of college life." [31]

But regardless of whether a woman attended a coeducational institution or whether she was predisposed to marriage, Carey Thomas was adamant in her insistence that all women should prepare for self-support. She loathed images of complacent, submissive wives and mothers and felt that college women who married would presumably prefer to do other work in order to be able to pay wages to have what she considered household drudgery done for them. And, characteristically employing the same standards for men as for women, she wrote: "No college-bred man would be willing day after day to shovel coal in his cellar, or to curry and harness his horses, if by more intellectual and interesting labor he could earn enough to pay to have it done for him." [32] One Bryn Mawr woman, having repeatedly been warned by President Thomas against the greatest evil—complacent wifehood—wrote in a book of reminiscences published by her class that "just to prove that though married, I am not a useless frivolous creature—I am Reader in German at the Central High School." Another graduate wrote: "Next year I will be one more added to Miss Thomas' notable list of those married *and* employed." [33]

But most notable to Thomas were her beloved scholars to whom she did not even sanction the option of marriage. At Bryn Mawr commencements she reserved her highest praise for those women who planned to continue their studies in graduate schools. She particularly lauded those who would travel abroad, sacrificing all personal pleasures that might await them in America for a chance to study with a revered professor in a well-known European university. Her speeches to Bryn Mawr students reiterated again and again the altruistic satisfactions they would receive in sacrificing their lives to advancing "the bounds of human knowledge," not to mention the bounds of women's achievements. Her writings and talks stressing equality and congeniality between the sexes that would be spurred by women's higher education were saved mainly for the world outside Bryn Mawr College, for she had wished to encourage as many of her students as possible to lead lives of "intellectual renunciation" and "sex solidarity."

Thomas's belief that Bryn Mawr College would remain an isolated training ground for a new breed of woman reveals her faith in the power of the collegiate experience to mold lifetime careers and ambitions. She saw herself as capable of producing a new female specialty which would have the strength to compete successfully with men in a controlled arena. Yet, in trying to carve a sphere for women's excellence, she ignored—and would have her students ignore—the larger social context that was the source of the inequality. The limitations both of collegiate instruction and the insularity Thomas insisted upon would inevitably become clear to her. She could never make a connection with the outside world without some conflict and dissonance resulting; she could not expect her students to maintain her posture. Inevitably, Thomas's orthodoxy deteriorated, largely under the pressure of outside opinion which insisted upon female specialties that were in tune with domesticity. It would take more than one institution standing alone to make such alternative actions possible.

By about 1910 her rhetoric began to change, and she was telling her students that it might indeed be possible for women to successfully combine marriage and an academic career: "The next advance in women's education is then to throw open to the competition of women scholars the rewards and prizes of a scholar's life and to allow women professors like men professors to marry, or not, as they see fit." [34] "Allowing" her venerated women scholars to marry and "join the few men of genius in their generation in the service of their common race" [35] was, for Thomas, a major revision in her professed beliefs.

But of even more significance was her increasing de-emphasis on the scholar as the most "precious beyond all other human products." [36] In more and more speeches after 1910 she spoke nostalgically of intellectual preoccupations as if they were remnants of another generation—a generation that she felt part of. She reminisced about long afternoons and evenings that students would devote to "voracious and limitless reading of poetry and unending discussions of abstract questions among themselves." [37] The poets and popular novelists in her day—Wordsworth, Shelley, Keats, Browning, George Eliot, and Balzac—seemed unacceptable to a generation who admired Kipling and Tolstoi. She wrote: "The students of today are interested in what they believe to be very modern and practical studies, apparently without regard to the relative teaching ability of the professors. Students often say to me that they wish to study these subjects because, as they say, they will help them to deal with life, and it is dealing with life that they are eager for." [38]

Carey Thomas, who had never before considered introducing so-called practical and modern courses into the staunchly classical and rigorous Bryn Mawr curriculum, was now forced to reevaluate the programs of study as well as her own ideals about the model Bryn Mawr graduate. By 1910 a whole new generation of students was entering women's colleges—students for whom the college experience was not unique. The mission-oriented student who, convinced of her specialness, came to Bryn Mawr prepared to be swayed by Thomas's calls to advance the dignity of women through careers in research and academia was largely replaced by students who were impatient with the irrelevance of academic life. They looked outward to find rewarding relationships and to seek careers that would not be so isolating.

And, by 1910, new careers for college women were very much the topic of discussion in such forums as the Association of Collegiate Alumnae (later known as the American Association of University Women) and in the colleges themselves. As more and more women attended college, they saw their collective experience as providing ways of solving problems about occupations and life styles rather than as supplying them with already defined alternatives. Students entering college must certainly have been aware of talk about careers for women in social work and domestic economy, which, because of the new technological emphasis, were given applied scientific status. Such areas as sanitary science, domestic science, and hygiene began to appear as courses of study in some women's colleges. Careers in social reform for women were not new; women such as Alice Palmer had urged students to pursue charitable work thirty years before. But her notions about this work were vague; she seemed to see women scurrying from one cause to another, aiding in whatever capacity they were needed. Now, however, careers became more clearly defined and professionalized. Entering Bryn Mawr students, who saw no evidence of these courses and emphases in their curriculum, must surely have begun to pressure Carey Thomas to awaken to the new phenomena.[39]

Thomas, however, always sensitive to the possible degradation of women, must have feared that these new careers were merely an attempt to professionalize traditional areas of acceptability for women. Therefore, in responding to demands for change, she tried to incorporate some of these new concerns without sacrificing too much of the intellectual rigor. Courses in social work were introduced on the graduate level— although undergraduates could elect some of them—and the emphasis was more on sociology than on applied science. In addition, through her speeches, she tried to remove the shroud of feminine gentility so often associated with social work and asked her students to march boldly to the rescue, confronting the "stupendous weight of crime and misery." [40]

She also stressed that social reform should be the task of both men and women, who must join together to fight injustice.

By about 1910 Carey Thomas had retreated from extolling sex solidarity and had begun to advocate congeniality between the sexes. Furthermore, she shifted from promoting isolating scholarly pursuits to praising careers aimed at "social reconstruction and human betterment." [41] Much of the vehemence that she had displayed in lauding scholarly careers was now transferred to careers in social reform. In dramatic language, previously reserved exclusively for prospective scholars, she proclaimed to graduating Bryn Mawr students:

> You are the children of your generation, the generation on whom will rest the heavy civic responsibilities which our generation turned aside. We confidently believe that your Bryn Mawr education will have fitted you to meet them. The hope of social reform lies with the young men and women leaving college to enter into active life. As I have tried to show in my address, a thousand voices are calling you to this great work—We bid you God's speed.[42]

Thomas's rhetoric changed over time; her struggle for women's dignity became less solitary as she brought it outside of academia and Bryn Mawr into the social realm of men and women. Her own life seemed to be altered, for she began to look beyond the academic world of Bryn Mawr and gave vigorous support to the suffrage, prohibition, and international peace movements. Yet she berated those women—and men—who saw social reform as being inherently suitable for women with their more refined moral sensibilities, and continued to call for women's educational circumstances to be the same as those for men. She remained adamant about the necessity that women refuse to bow to subservience, and she urged them to become both economically and psychologically independent.

NOTES

1. Hugh Hawkins, *Between Harvard and America: The Educational Leadership of Charles W. Eliot* (New York, 1972), p. 289.

2. Charles W. Eliot, *The Man and His Beliefs* (New York, 1923), p. 575.

3. Ibid., p. 167.

4. Ibid.

5. Laurence R. Veysey, "Martha Carey Thomas," in *Notable American Women*, ed. Edward T. James, vol. 3 (Cambridge, Mass., 1971), p. 448. Veysey's succinct account of Thomas is a very insightful, balanced portrait that contrasts to most

posthumous writing on Thomas—which is overwhelmingly positive and sees her as *the* pioneer of women's higher education.

6. Martha Carey Thomas, "Notes for the Opening Address at Bryn Mawr College," Bryn Mawr College Archives, 1899. This address is unusual, for she did not often use the Bryn Mawr College forum for such vehement and specific attacks.

7. Martha Carey Thomas, "Should the Higher Education of Women Differ from That of Men?" *Educational Review* 21 (1901): 5.

8. See Martha Carey Thomas, "The Future of Women in Independent Study and Research," Publications of the Association of Collegiate Alumnae, Series 3, Number 6 (February 1903). Although she most often spoke of the value of independent research, she realized that most women would need further means of support and, therefore, advocated university teaching as well.

9. Quoted in Edith Finch, *Carey Thomas of Bryn Mawr* (New York, 1947), p. 87. There is some rich material on Thomas's early life in this biography, but the end tends to deteriorate into an apology for Thomas's administration at Bryn Mawr.

10. Barbara Cross, *The Educated Woman in America* (New York, 1965), p. 31. The primary source material on Thomas that Cross presents is very illustrative of the change in her rhetoric which is discussed later in this chapter.

11. Quoted in Finch, p. 36.

12. Cross, p. 32.

13. It is difficult to provide a social class analysis of women college students of this period without knowing fathers' occupations. There are some indications, though, that most students came from middle- to upper middle-class families—probably daughters of professionals or business people. Tuition with room and board was high in comparison to average salaries of the time. At Bryn Mawr, families paid $350 a year in 1885; by 1889 the fee had gone up to $400. If, in 1885, a well-paid high school principal made $2500 a year, he would have to scrimp and save to send his daughter to college. Scholarships were offered, but in the early years of low endowments not too many students had an opportunity to attend at a reduced rate. College did not become fashionable for upper-class women until well into the twentieth century. Most often, as is indicated here, they would be trooped off to Europe to become sufficiently cultivated marriage partners. Too much classical education was not deemed to be womanly. The European tour was made by many young American women—among them Jane Addams whose stepmother, who was responsible for the trip, was of a prominent family. Addams, of course, was not a typical "neurasthenic" woman (to use Christopher Lasch's phrase). She graduated from a seminary which had officially become a college at the time of her graduation and she would use the European junket for quite different purposes than most. See Jane Addams, *Twenty Years at Hull House.* (New York, 1910)—especially the chapter entitled "The Snare of Preparation." See also Allen F. Davis, *American Heroine, The Life and Legend of Jane Addams* (New York, 1971), ch. 2.

14. Cross, p. 34. See also Logan Pearsall Smith's *Unforgotten Years* (Boston, 1938).

15. Ibid.

16. Ibid.

17. Quoted in Morris Bishop, *A History of Cornell* (Ithaca, New York, 1962), p. 147.

18. Ibid., p. 151.

19. Finch, p. 87.

20. Thomas, "Notes for the Opening Address at Bryn Mawr College."

21. Thomas, "Should the Higher Education of Women Differ from That of Men?," p. 1.

22. Thomas, "Present Tendencies in Women's College and University Education," *Educational Review* 25 (1908): 83.

23. Ibid.

24. Martha Carey Thomas, "The Future of Women's Higher Education," *Mount Holyoke College: The Seventy-fifth Anniversary* (South Hadley, Mass., 1913), pp. 100-104.

25. The issue of whether Thomas's relationships with close women friends assumed a sexual character is the subject of part of a recent rather gossipy history of the Seven Sister schools—Elaine Kendall, *Peculiar Institutions: An Informal History of the Seven Sister Colleges* (New York, 1975, 1976). The obsession with this issue dwells on the irrelevant; what is important is the way her notion of sex separation became translated to students and to college policy.

26. Thomas, "Should the Higher Education. . . ," p. 10.

27. Ibid.

28. Ibid.

29. Martha Carey Thomas, "The College Women of the Present and Future," 1901, Bryn Mawr College Archives.

30. Martha Carey Thomas, "Education of Women," in *Monographs on Education in the United States,* ed. Nicholas Murray Butler (New York, 1899), p. 358.

31. Ibid.

32. Thomas, "Present Tendencies. . . ," p. 82.

33. Bulletins of the Class of 1916, comments by Zelda Branch Cramer and Marion Brown, Bryn Mawr College Archives.

34. Thomas, "The Future of Women's Higher Education," p. 102.

35. Thomas, "Present Tendencies. . . ," p. 85.

36. Ibid.

37. Martha Carey Thomas, "Notes for Commencement Address at Bryn Mawr College, June 6, 1907," Bryn Mawr College Archives.

38. Ibid. These words sound all too familiar and are, indeed, part of the progressive rhetoric. As much recent scholarship on progressivism has shown, the "life adjustment" movement often was a catchword for social control; and conservative purposes were evident in some of the most radical-sounding ideals. See Christopher Lasch, *The New Radicalism in America* (New York, 1965), pp. 13-14 for a discussion of this idea in reference to Jane Addams. It is clear that women's turn toward social work careers—at least on a rhetorical level—was part of this whole mentality. See Chapter VI.

39. For evidence of this see Bryn Mawr College Bulletins, Class of 1916, Bryn
Mawr College Archives, especially the statement of Isabel Vincent Harper.
40. Thomas, "Notes for Commencement Address. . . ,"
41. Ibid.
42. Ibid.

CHAPTER III

Alice Freeman Palmer
and the Wellesley Woman

Alice Freeman Palmer died suddenly in 1902 at age 47, and many Americans mourned the death of an exceptional woman. Charles Eliot was among the most effusive of the eulogists, calling her the most perfect example of American womanhood to date.[1] At a meeting held to plan memorials of Palmer's life and work, Eliot, who presided, spoke of her total commitment to the ideal of service—service to her family as well as to countless boys and girls and men and women throughout the country.[2]

Eliot's response to Alice Palmer varied considerably from his opinion of Carey Thomas, whose abrupt, unfeminine manner and unorthodox stance were repugnant to him. But although Alice Palmer was just as committed to the higher education of talented women as was Thomas, their goals for college women were not the same. Palmer, like Eliot, believed in the natural differentiation of complementary functions between the sexes and felt that the so-called normal propensities of both men and women should be fully developed. Unlike Eliot, however, Palmer's lines of demarcation were never so sharp that she could not praise certain unusual women who were able to find happiness and success as lawyers, doctors, or chemists. But her basic orientation was to encourage women to excel in "characteristic employments of housekeeping, teaching, and ministering to the afflicted."[3]

Palmer's adulation of the family, and her desire that women should extend the context of the home by becoming society's moral benefactors were highly acceptable ideas to most nineteenth-century Americans who, like Eliot, were horrified by Carey Thomas's sexless scholar who would compete with men and shun domesticity. Palmer would use education to further these ideas; a woman's intellectual training would make her capable of more direct and rational action as she worked tirelessly for various social causes. Her training would also assure her of a richer marriage: "Yet even if that which is the profession of women par excellence be hers, how can she be perennially so interesting a companion to her husband and children as if she had keen personal tastes, long her own, and growing with her growth?" [4]

When Carey Thomas publicly defended higher education for women on the grounds that it would enable men and women to live together as comrades, her rhetoric must have sounded hollow to those who also heard her speak of sex solidarity. Indeed, her words might have been deemed expedient: she sought to counterbalance hysterical cries that college-educated women were acquiring an Amazonian coarseness and were becoming anemic and incapable of maternal feeling.[5] Alice Palmer's similar statements, however, were far from empty and could not be construed as defensive, since both her words and actions at Wellesley testify to her belief that a prime function of a woman's college was to build up a woman's character, consisting primarily of heightened moral sensibilities, by imparting simple tastes and generous sympathies. "Learning alone is not enough for women," [6] she said.

It is evident that Alice Freeman Palmer was within the mainstream of acceptable responses to domesticity by women in education. She clearly tried to adapt an entrenched set of values to a new institution. Yet the nature of the institution itself—imparting a so-called higher education to its students—had some effect upon the transmission of these traditional values. In college, girls would be subjected not only to attempts at character building but also to a steady routine of strenuous mental work. This combination would not necessarily produce a woman whose ambitions stopped at conversing intelligently with her husband or attending to charitable causes in her leisure time. Her ambitions might exceed those designed for her by the college leaders, and she might choose to emphasize the intellectual aspect of her training at the expense of the domestic.

Alice Palmer did not wish considerations of the intellect to take priority over considerations of sex. Rather, she sought to combine noble womanhood with intellect and create what John Rousmanière has called a "cultural hybrid." [7] Such a woman would be neither sexless nor overly delicate, but would be intensely moral, sensitive, and refined as well as disciplined and rational. Palmer hoped that the negative qualities associated with femininity—such as wearisome caprice and pettiness—and those associated with sexless intellectuality—such as crudity and insensitivity—might disappear in these "strong, high-minded, generous, courageous spirits." [8] If Carey Thomas considered her scholar a unique and exceptional breed, Alice Palmer had nothing but the highest praise for her noble, graceful, articulate woman who would primarily concern herself with her home and with educational or charitable enterprises. The scholar might advance the bounds of human knowledge, but the dignified, disciplined woman would insure the progress of civilization by molding the character of future men and women and by caring for the downtrodden. Therefore, it was not overly grandiose to proclaim that: "The civilization of the Anglo-Saxon race depends upon the education—physical, mental, moral, and social—of the women for the next fifty years." [9]

The "cultural hybrid," however, had certain problems attached to her unique status. Most significantly, she had to assume a delicate balance between womanliness and intellect without overemphasizing either trait. Such a creature was easy to create rhetorically, but in practice it was difficult to achieve such a state of equilibrium, except perhaps in the controlled college environment. Ambivalence and conflict were bound to accompany attempts to achieve this vulnerable but very high status. Martha Carey Thomas's idealized scholar may also have been difficult to reproduce in reality, but at least "her expectations had not been raised by a faith in the ultimate compatibility of true womanhood and sexless intellect." [10] For the Bryn Mawr woman, only marriage and sexual needs—which the truly disciplined woman could control—stood between the educated woman and high achievement. But for Palmer's model, there was no clear-cut formula for success, as inherently antithetical elements had to be synthesized in one personality.

Alice Palmer certainly recognized this duality and spoke of it directly. Interestingly, she occasionally referred to the "human side," by which she meant the intellect, versus the "woman side"—a distinction that Carey Thomas would have found appalling. Like Thomas, Alice Palmer was ambivalent on the question of coeducation; but her ambivalence stemmed from this conflict between womanliness and intellect and not from any conflicting thoughts about equality versus isolationism and elitism. For Palmer, as for Charles Eliot, ideas about equality and supremacy were meaningless; both saw the functions of the sexes as dissimilar yet complementary. In an article in which she summarized ideas on the relative merits of coeducation versus women's colleges,

Alice Freeman Palmer spoke of both atmospheres as having their strengths and weaknesses. Coeducation, she believed, would provide a stimulating atmosphere where intellectual facilities would be fully developed. She cited her own experience at the University of Michigan as an example of an education filled with academic challenge. Women's colleges might not provide such thorough intellectual training: "At any rate, whatever may be thought of the relative importance of the two sides—the woman side and the human side—it will be generally agreed that the training of the young woman is apt to be peculiarly weak in agencies for bringing home to her the importance of direct and rational action." [11] But no system could meet every need of a woman's nature, and coeducation could never adequately provide for those exclusively feminine qualities such as graces of manner, niceties of speech and dress, and shy delicacy.[12] And certainly "the exercise of her special function of motherhood demands sheltered circumstances and refined moral perceptions." [13]

It was hard to imagine a woman of refined tastes and shy delicacy being at the same time capable of direct and forceful action. Alice Palmer herself had difficulty in merging these elements in her own personality without conflict. Indeed, she seemed to mask her own ambivalence until a crisis such as her agonizing decision whether or not to marry forced her to face her accumulation of power and her lack of shy delicacy as Wellesley's president. Once confronted with the option to marry, she was reluctant to give up her position and often visualized marriage as the other extreme—total "surrender" to the quiet, womanly life. Thus, she had difficulty in visualizing the combination of elements in her own life which she sought to create in her students.

Yet after she was married she did live up to her image of the noble disciplined woman who, with her home as a base, used her leisure time to pursue many educational and charitable causes actively. She retained contact with Wellesley as a trustee, was on the Massachusetts Board of Education, and was very active in several woman's educational organizations. It is perhaps doubtful if she would have been able to pursue such activities had not her reputation as Wellesley's president preceded her entry into married life. Yet she believed that marriage brought with it the kind of serenity and security that most women needed in order to live a varied and useful life. In a speech before the American Institute of Instruction in 1885, Alice Freeman prefaced her remarks by saying that one must never ask what becomes of a girl's education if she marries. She went on to talk about a successful and beautiful college professor who resigned her position to be the wife of a businessman in a lumber town. Before she left the college, she said she would be going to broader and more important work; she would help to make the town a center of good influence, a city of importance.[14] Alice Palmer would certainly have agreed with Caroline Hazard's opinion of her decision, stated after the former's death: "It seems to me proof of the growth of her life that she left all this at Wellesley, which had been so largely the work of her own hands and heart, and found a larger usefulness in her marriage. She laid down one specific work to take up a dozen others, and the sunshine of her home touched many a life with glory." [15] Yet, with the "hybridization" of her personality, she never again achieved the power and stature that she had held at Wellesley.

Alice Palmer's decision to marry was perhaps inevitable, given her continued insistence on the sanctity of marriage and motherhood. She did have priorities, and, when faced with a choice, was willing to consider the duties of a wife and mother above all else for herself as well as for other women to whom she gave advice. When asked by the American Woman Suffrage Association to give her opinion on the vote for women, she replied that she was in favor of suffrage. But her reasons reveal her commitment to the image of women as wives and mothers as well as her belief in the importance of such roles:

It cannot be shown that there are any large number of women in this country who have not the necessary time to vote intelligently. Study of the vital questions of our government would make them better comrades to their husbands and friends, better comrades to their sons, and more interesting members of society. . . . The duties of motherhood and the making of the home are the most sacred work of women, and the dearest to them, of every class. If casting an intelligent vote would interfere with what women only can do—and what, failed in, undermines society and government—no one can question which a woman must choose.[16]

Alice Palmer's ideal woman, then, would spend a large portion of her time intelligently serving the needs of her home and family. In addition, she would make worthy use of leisure time by ministering to the young and afflicted. In a speech before the Association of Collegiate Alumnae, she spoke of women as "the only class that is a leisure class"; because of their leisure, she hoped that college women could assume management of philanthropical and educational associations which "overworked fathers and brothers are putting into our hands." [17] This speech is important because it emphasizes Palmer's notion of a leisure class. She ignored the essential fact that a leisure class is not self-supporting, and, thus, could not be independently conceived. She hinted at this dependency when she talked of fathers and brothers putting charitable work "into our hands." Yet she attempted to fashion a female speciality which would balance the intellect and domesticity away from fathers and brothers in the relative isolation of the college campus. She kept discussions about women's roles introverted, making it appear as if social and political considerations were not forcing her hand in any way. It is true, however, that the dependent woman who was committed to the sanctity of marriage above all else served the agenda of "fathers and brothers." And it was they, more than college women, that dictated the female speciality.

Palmer's appeal to women to enter charitable occupations was based on more than the issue of leisure time. She was an intensely moral woman and wished to develop a moral purity and a sense of divine mission in her students which would inspire them to serve humanity. In speeches—resembling Carey Thomas's cadenced calls to tackle social responsibilities that she made in the later part of her career—Alice Palmer summoned her own students to reform society. Unlike Thomas, however, Palmer did not see social work as a joint venture for men and women. She saw such work as a natural release for women's inherently heightened moral perceptions. College might refine such natural perceptions further and provide the intellectual resources for more rational and forthright actions, but the basic raw material was already there and was expressed in terms of womanly qualities. Thomas refused to ascribe connotations of womanliness to social reform; that would have, in her eyes, denigrated the achievements that she was calling upon women to make. Neither Palmer nor Thomas saw social reform as a genteel activity. But whereas Thomas refused to shroud it in a feminine context, preferring instead to give it—like the life of intellectual renunciation—a sexless character, Palmer was very much conscious of its particular suitability for women.

It was Palmer's rather than Thomas's conception of the woman's role in social reform that was both consistent with tradition and most palatable to later generations of college women. Alice Palmer had talked vaguely about extending the use of a woman's moral sensibilities into the wide social arena. Future women educators would refine and specify the various fields of social work that college graduates with their intellectual training might find suitable.

Alice Palmer and Carey Thomas were contemporaries and respected each other's accomplishments. However, they differed in their attitudes toward proper female roles. And, as the next two chapters will indicate, these differences were not merely rhetorical; they were manifested in the types of institutions Palmer and Thomas helped to shape, for these women's administrations were intensely personal and reflected their own life experience. It was at least partially because of this intermingling between personal and professional roles that these women, despite their ideological differences, had something important in common. Thomas's celibate scholar and Palmer's "cultural hybrid" were products of each woman's attempts to deal with her own expectations. Thus, they—and Thomas in particular—did not look to the outside, but tried to create an environment where they themselves would fashion their particular brand of educated women. These isolated images of the collegiate woman would not survive, in large part because "outside forces," primarily in the form of university men, began to use public arenas, including women's own organizations, to spell out their views of the proper uses of women's higher education. Thomas's scholar all but disappeared; Palmer's "cultural hybrid" became diluted as new careers were found that integrated the two parts, and in so doing resolved all the conflicts, creating a far more bland image of the educated woman.

NOTES

1. Charles Eliot, quoted in "Personal Recollections of Alice Freeman Palmer—Milwaukee, November 7, 1903," *Collegiate Alumnae Magazine* (February 1904).

2. Charles Eliot, quoted in "Record of a Meeting Held at Boston on December 29, 1902 to Plan for Memorials for the Life and Work of Alice Freeman Palmer," *Publications of the Association of Collegiate Alumnae* (1903).

3. Alice Freeman Palmer, "Women's Education at the World's Fair," in *The Teacher: Essays and Addresses on Education* by George Herbert Palmer and Alice Freeman Palmer (Boston, 1908), p. 362. Most of this volume is devoted to George Herbert Palmer's philosophical discussion about teaching; a small section at the end contains Alice Palmer's few published pieces. According to George Palmer, Mrs. Palmer avoided writing, thinking that "her work was best accomplished by spoken words" (p. 310).

4. Alice Freeman Palmer, "Why Go to College," *The Teacher: Essays and Addresses on Education*, p. 380.

5. This particular sentiment—about Amazonian coarseness and anemia—and others of the same caliber are found in Edward A. Clarke's *Sex in Education—or A Fair Chance for the Girls* (Boston, 1873). The book was immensely popular and caused friends of women's higher education to publish defenses (see note 6) showing how college education was compatible with femininity and marriage. It also helped spark a deep concern about health of college women. Women's colleges—partly as a result—provided plenty of time and facility for proper exercise. Later the Association of Collegiate Alumnae sponsored an elaborate study in which they tried to prove statistically that the health of college women was not only excellent but better than that of noncollege women.

48   COLLEGIATE WOMEN

6. Alice Freeman Palmer, "A Review of the Higher Education of Women," in *Women and the Higher Education,* ed. Anna Brackett (New York, 1893), p. 119. Anna Brackett (1836–1911), the editor of this collection of essays on women's education, worked primarily in public schools and normal schools, but she was also a staunch defender of college education for women. Many of her articles and poems—some of them about higher education—appeared in popular magazines of the day such as *Harper's.* In 1874 she published *The Education of American Girls,* which was designed to be a response to Edward Clarke's book, published the year before.

7. John P. Rousmanière, "Cultural Hybrid in the Slums: The College Woman and the Settlement House, 1889–94," *Education in American History—Readings on the Social Issues,* ed. Michael Katz (New York, 1973), pp. 122–38.

8. Palmer, "Why Go to College," p. 385.

9. Alice Freeman Palmer, "Influence of Women's Education on National Character," *American Institute of Instruction Proceedings,* 1885.

10. Rousmanière, p. 137.

11. Palmer, "A Review of the Higher Education of Women," p. 114.

12. Ibid.

13. Ibid.

14. Palmer, "Influence of Women's Education on National Character," p. 170.

15. Caroline Hazard, speech at the Memorial Service for Alice Freeman Palmer, Appleton Chapel, Harvard University, January 31, 1903. Reprinted in Caroline Hazard, *From College Gates* (Boston, 1925), p. 191. Caroline Hazard became president of Wellesley in 1899; she and Alice Palmer were friends and shared many of the same views about the social uses of women's higher education. Hazard's administration, like Palmer's, was an exceptional one: the former more than tripled the endowment, allowing the solidification of a costly elective system. See Margaret Clapp, "Caroline Hazard," in *Notable American Women,* ed. Edward T. James, vol. 1 (Cambridge, Mass., 1971).

16. National American Woman Suffrage Association, Political Equality Series, *Eminent Opinions on Woman Suffrage,* statements by Alice Freeman Palmer, p. 28.

17. Alice Freeman Palmer, speech before the Association of Collegiate Alumnae, ACA Publications, Series III, Number 5 (February 1902), p. 41. Note how the characterization of leisure is exactly that of her husband referring later to the distinctive feature of her married life in the *Life of Alice Freeman Palmer.*

CHAPTER IV

The Years of Definition:
Bryn Mawr and Wellesley, 1885-1908

"The Bryn Mawr woman gazes with the most unconcerned indifference, even semi-contemptuousness at the 'Haverford *boys*,' with a very small b, and speaks of Princeton College as the Bryn Mawr annex!" [1] The Bryn Mawr woman—dubbed Bryn Mawrter by nostalgic graduates—belonged to an aristocracy of wit and brains, for only those with very superior intellectual facility could pass the rigorous entrance examinations required of all applicants.

Although M. Carey Thomas did not actually become head of Bryn Mawr College until 1894, when President James Rhoades died, her influence on the infant college was marked from the beginning. As dean of the faculty and professor of English, she was Rhoades's closest associate, and he looked to her for guidance and direction. Her father and uncle, as well as several family friends, were on the Board of Trustees and could generally be counted upon to support Thomas's proposals. From the beginning she refused to allow any educational adulteration at Bryn Mawr, hoping to create an atmosphere conducive to the development of her idealized scholar.

According to the first *Bryn Mawr College Program*, published in 1885, all prospective students were required to pass either the Harvard University entrance examination or to take another difficult examination given by Bryn Mawr College, in which they had to demonstrate competence in

49

TABLE 1
Preparatory Study for
Admission to Bryn Mawr [1]

Classes of	1889–93	1894–98	1899–1903	1904–8	Total
Private school	22–73%	28–78%	34–55%	46–64%	130–65%
High school	2– 7%	6–17%	16–26%	20–28%	44–22%
Privately tutored	2– 7%	2– 6%	4– 6%	2– 3%	10– 5%
College [2]	4–13%	–	8–13%	4– 6%	16– 8%
Total sample	30	36	62	72	200

[1] based upon a 20 percent sample of Bryn Mawr college graduates taken from Bryn Mawr college alumnae registers.

[2] Students in this category attended another college for a short time first. Most often this college did not have the rigorous course of study that Bryn Mawr had. Therefore, they were generally admitted to Bryn Mawr as entering freshmen rather than as transfer students.

such disciplines as Greek, Latin, and mathematics. Unlike most other women's colleges, Bryn Mawr never had an affiliated preparatory department which allowed unqualified students to be accepted on the condition that they prepare for admission into the regular college. Therefore, the twenty-four young women who entered the first class of Bryn Mawr College in 1885 were all highly competent students.

Most of the women in Bryn Mawr's early classes had attended private schools (Table 1). At such exclusive and fashionable institutions as Miss Gibbons' in New York, the girls would be saturated with Latin and trigonometry and trained in tea pouring and flower arranging as well. For many of the students, the intellectual training did nothing but help them to land successful, enterprising husbands, and their graceful adornments stood them in good stead as they prepared to devote their lives to their husbands, and, eventually, to their children. Perhaps they might occasionally venture from the hearthside to join a group of women engaged in charitable efforts to improve public schools or to aid destitute children.

M. Carey Thomas insisted that students reside at the college. Residence at a self-contained community would, she believed, stave off the influence of the outside world. She wrote: "No such type can possibly be created except by a residence college and unless carefully divided like Oxford and Cambridge into resident halls a very large college loses the power to mould its students in external ways." [2] Bryn Mawr was divided into residence halls, and each hall was headed by a scholarly Bryn Mawr College graduate who was studying for an advanced degree. According to Helen Thomas Flexner, who graduated from Bryn Mawr in 1893, such older, more serious students had a strong influence on the undergraduates in their halls.[3] Thomas assumed that the correlation between isolation with proper living arrangements and avoidance of intellectual stagnation would be almost automatic. This belief was central to her plan for managing the lives of her students. It was, though, self-defeating in the end—first, because it ignored the weighing of outside social pressures after graduation, pressures which her students would feel against their living a life of "intellectual renunciation." Moreover, Thomas, in stressing the importance of on-campus living arrangements in developing her model scholar, avoided really specific discussions about concrete characteristics of intellectual discipline. Thus, it was difficult to discern exactly how and when one achieved an acceptable status. But again, in Thomas's rhetoric it was the dramatic image making that prevailed. As in her own experience with scholarship, the substance mattered less than the resulting effect. Isolation at Bryn Mawr allowed Thomas at least the illusion of control; it also bolstered images of the elusive, intellectual student that Thomas sought to fashion.

And she did attempt, within Bryn Mawr's closed doors, to give students a strong dose of classical training with a minimum of diversion. Most women's colleges in the late nineteenth century required students to care for their rooms as well as to participate in the general domestic work of the college. Such a requirement was less a result of financial need than an opportunity to train future wives and mothers in household management. Bryn Mawr shunned this concession to domesticity, and the catalogue testified to this policy: "No part whatever need be taken by the student in the care of her own room." [4] It was expected that almost all spare time would be used for academic purposes. The curriculum as well as aspects of student life were modeled after the finest men's colleges, where no student would ever be asked to help with the maintenance of the college.

Indeed, Bryn Mawr was sometimes jokingly called "Janes Hopkins," because the group system, which Johns Hopkins imported from German universities, was in effect at Bryn Mawr. The appellation was quite acceptable to Thomas. The group system insured that students would have a strong foundation in general disciplinary subjects as well as in several areas of special research. A minimum of electives was permitted. M. Carey Thomas was adamant about stressing the so-called "old-fashioned" disciplines, such as Greek, higher mathematics, and philosophy; these, she felt, could best train the mental faculties. She said—again using dramatic imagery: "A woman's college is a place where we take those wonderful, tender and innocent freshmen with their inherited prejudices and ancestral emotions and mould them by four years of strenuous intellectual discipline into glorious thinking, reasoning women fit to govern themselves and others." [5] She would not countenance including "frivolous" subjects such as music and drawing, which were central to women's seminaries and were part of most women's colleges, in the curriculum. Not only did these pursuits smack of feminine gentility; they also failed to provide the necessary intellectual discipline: "Drawing, painting, instrumental music, domestic science, library work, typewriting, steno, shopwork, manual training have no place whatever in a college course such as I am describing because they do not give the kind of mental work that should be given by college studies." [6] Only courses in architecture, or in the history of art, were tolerated, since they had the potential to develop into disciplinary subjects.

Thomas always chose faculty with the utmost care. Most of the members were men, because it was impossible for her to find enough qualified women to fill the ranks. Alvin Johnson, who taught at Bryn Mawr, remembered Carey Thomas as a majestic woman whose speech, dignity, and classical style reminded him of a passage from Sophocles. Such a manner was befitting Bryn Mawr's curriculum and the aura that surrounded the campus—an aura that Carey Thomas not only reflected but was instrumental in creating. She demanded excellence, and it was said that if a man was not good enough to be called to a post at a great university within seven years, she fired him. According to Johnson: "She never lost a man, she used to say, without replacing him with a better one." [7]

Underneath the dignified classical aura, Bryn Mawr was infused with a competitive and often tense atmosphere, also engendered by Thomas. She wished to prepare her students to compete for positions, particularly in academia; in order to enter the struggle, they had to be used to tough competition and rigorous academic demands. Cultural veneer combined with scholastic prowess and a keen competitive sense were key elements in the personality that Carey Thomas sought to develop.

Most students met with Thomas alone only occasionally and the subject was most often academics. According to the program of 1895, when Thomas became president: "Each student is expected to consult the President in regard to the details and best arrangements of her various studies." [8] It was Thomas's desire, then, to oversee her students' academic life from the beginning. Later in her college career, the Bryn

Mawr student's contact with Carey Thomas would usually be limited to morning chapel, where Thomas would give incisive talks on the splendor of the scholarly life. To her, "the intellectual life was an exalted end to be pursued with all the strength that the spirit possessed." [9] Grades were always posted after examinations, and Carey Thomas rebuked professors whose grades were uniformly high. The most dreaded exam was the senior oral or the final language examination. The student would present herself in full academic dress to the president and two faculty members. She would then be required to translate quickly and accurately French and German passages from sight. It was a dreaded experience,[10] but despite student protest, Carey Thomas did not modify the examination for many years. According to Thomas, the ordeal was extremely worthwhile, for it tested both scholarship and discipline, qualities essential for the successful Bryn Mawr student.

Extracurricular activities and nonacademic events seemed only to reinforce both the competitiveness and refined cultural aura surrounding the campus. Physical exercise was not advocated at Bryn Mawr merely because of the belief that women's health would suffer from too much academia; rather, sports were pursued with a vigor that was consuming for both participants and spectators. It was a calamity, wrote Helen Thomas Flexner, when Bryn Mawr lost a basketball championship.[11] A Self Government Association was formed and canvasses for office were often exciting, diverting, and again, very competitive. However, decisions were always subject to Carey Thomas's approval. Other activities and events of a more reflective nature combined high culture with a certain elitism that was so infusive at Bryn Mawr. Teas were a common occurrence in late afternoon. Girls would dress in caps and gowns and drop in to various college sitting rooms where conversations would range from English literature to politics. At dinner someone would be appointed to lead a conversation—usually on a scholarly topic. A "House of Commons" was organized which also provided a forum for discussion, particularly of a political nature.[12] Bryn Mawr students often were able to get a glimpse of the succession of notables invited to the college (for only those of eminence would be asked). Carey Thomas entertained them at the president's home, which was furnished with trappings from her summer sojourns around the world.

The Bryn Mawr student, then, was infected with a sense that she belonged to a very special society where only those of superior intellectual ability and cultural inclinations were invited. Her competitiveness often extended to contempt for male institutions. The Bryn Mawr College woman was aware of the mission for which she was being prepared. She would, if she remained true to Carey Thomas's very demanding hopes, lead a life devoted to scholarship, perhaps assuming a college teaching post. She would avoid strangulating marriages, and, in times of greatest stress, rely on members of her own sex for guidance.

At least until about 1910, Carey Thomas could be proud of many of her students' achievements. The intellectual life was pursued by 61 percent of all Bryn Mawr graduates between the years 1889 and 1908 [13] (Table 2). At a time when undergraduate education for women was so often criticized and graduate education was even less acceptable, such a figure is quite impressive. Occupational figures for graduates of Bryn Mawr during this period were also noteworthy. Only 10 percent of these women did not work during their lives. While most went into occupations that were already or rapidly becoming female-dominated, such as elementary school teaching and clerical work, a few became doctors and lawyers, and 10 percent of the graduates pursued a career in college teaching—a career that was, of course, of special significance to Carey Thomas (Table 3).

Of those Bryn Mawr women that graduated between 1889 and 1908, 47 percent married (Table 4). The rate is very low especially when compared to figures revealed in the 1910 census for the entire country. In that census, 88.6 percent of the female population between the ages of 35 and 44 were listed as married.[14]

The Bryn Mawr figures for marriage rate, occupation, and advanced study in this period are even more revealing when compared with statistical information for women who had a coeducational experience. During this same time period (1889-1908), few women who attended the University of Michigan went on for advanced study: 21 percent did so as compared with 61 percent of Bryn Mawr students (see Appendix, Table 1). Also, far fewer women from the University of Michigan had an occupation: 34 percent had one compared to 90 percent of Bryn Mawr students (see Appendix, Table 2). There was a smaller difference in marriage rates: 53 percent of Michigan students married, while the figure for Bryn Mawr was 47 percent (see Appendix, Table 3).

Other Bryn Mawr statistics for this period indicate that those who married did not necessarily have children; indeed, 32 percent did not (Table 5). But more significantly, 53 percent of married Bryn Mawr women who graduated between 1889 and 1908 had some kind of occupation during their marriage, and, thus, could have been economically self-sufficient (Table 6). It seems that some of these women managed to approach Carey Thomas's conception of the ideal union, where husband and career should coexist without the necessity of choice.

Students who attended Bryn Mawr in its early years were, it seems,

TABLE 2
Advanced Study of
Bryn Mawr Graduates [1,2]

Classes of	1889–93	1894–98	1899–1903	1904–8	Total
Advanced study					
MA	7–23%	2– 6%	6–10%	14–19%	29–14%
PhD	4–13%	1– 3%	4– 6%	–	9– 4%
MD, LLB, or JD	1– 3%	1– 3%	4– 6%	2– 3%	8– 4%
Advanced study/No degree [3]	11–37%	17–47%	22–35%	26–36%	76–38%
Subtotal	23–77%	21–58%	36–58%	42–58%	122–61%
No advanced study	7–23%	15–42%	26–42%	30–42%	78–39%
Total sample	30	36	62	72	200

[1] based upon a 20 percent sample of Bryn Mawr college graduates taken from Bryn Mawr college alumnae registers.

[2] In cases where alumnae received two degrees, the more advanced one was recorded.

[3] At least one year of study.

influenced by Carey Thomas's views. As a result of passing through the institution, many of these women were committed to a life where domestic values would not encroach on life styles or careers. Yet it is also true that some of these women came to Bryn Mawr prepared for the kind of bombardment that they would receive; their predisposition to Carey Thomas's attitudes helped to insure their successful socialization. As early college women they, as Carey Thomas herself, wished to escape lives of frivolity and saw the college as a way of refining and shaping their ambitions to defy a woman's usual lot. But they did not see how to come to terms with domesticity without rejecting all of the values associated with it. The extreme deviation was the response of a generation that did not as yet see alternative ways of dealing with the stagnation of domesticity except by remaining celibate, militant monuments to their discontent. More than this, the rejection of values associated with domesticity became, for some women, an almost evangelical state of mind rather than a mere inability to conceive of alternatives. Thomas herself falls into this category. Her rhetorical fervor, often heard in Bryn Mawr's chapel, seemed at times more the manner of a preacher than of a college president. And it was clearly this state of mind that she wished to transmit. The transformation from "tender, innocent freshmen" to "glorious, thinking, reasoning, women" would take place in an atmosphere at times appropriate to a religious revival.

TABLE 3
Occupations of Bryn Mawr
Graduates [1,2]

Classes of	1889–93	1894–98	1899–1903	1904–8	Total
Teaching/ tutoring	11–37%	15–42%	30–48%	22–31%	78–39%
College teaching	5–17%	5–14%	2– 3%	8–11%	20–10%
Clerical work	3–10%	—	4– 6%	10–14%	17– 8%
Social work	4–13%	9–25%	12–19%	12–17%	37–18%
Librarian	—	1– 3%	—	2– 3%	3– 1%
Doctor, lawyer	1– 3%	1– 3%	4– 6%	2– 3%	8– 4%
Other [3]	3–10%	2– 6%	6–10%	6– 8%	17– 8%
None	3–10%	3– 8%	4– 6%	10–14%	20–10%
Total sample	30	36	62	72	200

[1] based upon a 20 percent sample of Bryn Mawr college graduates taken from Bryn Maw college alumnae registers.

[2] Occupation listed is one which was pursued for the longest time.

[3] 1889–93 dairy farmer, housemother, editor; 1894–98 lab worker, industrial worker; 1899–1903 collector, government worker, missionary, milliner, editors (2); 1904–8 writers (2); nun, owner/manager of inn, farmer, editor.

TABLE 4
Marriage Rates of Bryn Mawr
Graduates [1,2]

Classes of	1889–93	1894–98	1899–1903	1904–8	Total
Married	13–43%	13–36%	36–58%	32–44%	94–47%
Unmarried	17–57%	23–64%	26–42%	40–56%	106–53%
Total sample	30	36	62	72	200

[1] based upon a 20 percent sample of Bryn Mawr college graduates taken from Bryn Mawr college alumnae registers.

[2] Statistics for these graduates were taken through 1938.

TABLE 5
Family Size of Married
Bryn Mawr Graduates

Number of Children Classes of	1889–93	1894–98	1899–1903	1904–8	Total
None	7–54%	5–38%	10–28%	8–25%	30–32%
One	1– 8%	—	8–22%	6–19%	15–16%
Two or three	5–38%	5–38%	10–28%	16–50%	36–38%
Four or more	—	3–23%	8–22%	2– 6%	13–14%
Total	13	13	36	32	94

Note: Includes all married Bryn Mawr graduates from Table 4.

TABLE 6
Relationship of Marriage and Occupation
of Bryn Mawr Graduates

Classes of	1889–93	1894–95	1899–1903	1904–8	Total
Occupation	7–54%	7–54%	18–50%	18–56%	50–53%
No occupation	6–46%	6–46%	18–50%	14–44%	44–47%
Total	13	13	36	32	94

Note: Includes all married Bryn Mawr college graduates from Table 4.

Bryn Mawr, then, was a college where—at least in its first twenty years—institutional development, ideology, and students' career and marriage patterns were coherently connected. The college represented a departure from traditional female educational institutions which sought to mold wives and mothers whose intellects would be subservient to domestic preoccupations. Carey Thomas tried to educate fiercely independent, competitive women who would not succumb to the passivity of being supported by a husband or to the stagnation of housework. The Bryn Mawr woman, who was bred in a mysterious shroud of gray stone Gothic buildings, and certainly President Thomas herself, were seen by outsiders as eccentric, elitist, unusually intelligent, but markedly undomesticated; in short, women who rejected all norms associated with submissive, servile femininity. Such characterizations witnessed the success of M. Carey Thomas in fulfilling her goals.

If Bryn Mawr swept away traditions of genteel female education, those who headed Wellesley College approached these same traditions with caution and ambivalence. The Wellesley woman was not often characterized in popular magazines as was her counterpart at Bryn Mawr, for her image, as well as that of the college, was elusive and less clearly defined.

When comparing statistical data for Wellesley College and Bryn Mawr, it becomes clear that there were differences between the two not only in image but also in career patterns of graduates.

Alumnae registers for Wellesley College included names of children and grandchildren as well as information about the graduate herself. Bryn Mawr bulletins focused only upon the graduate's own life. The type of data presented can be revealing of different institutional emphases; in the case of Bryn Mawr and Wellesley, these discrepancies are further corroborated by substantial statistical differences.

During the same twenty-year period—1889 to 1908—57 percent of all Wellesley graduates married (Table 7).[15] Although the figure is still considerably lower than that for the general population, it is higher by 10 percent than the figure for Bryn Mawr students. More married Wellesley graduates had children than Bryn Mawr graduates: 77 percent of Wellesley students had children (Table 8) as compared with 68 percent of those from Bryn Mawr.

Figures for advanced study and occupation show more marked differences. Of those Wellesley women who graduated between 1889 and 1908, 65 percent had no occupation listed in the registers while only 10 percent of Bryn Mawr students were in the same category (Table 9). The fact that 10 percent of Bryn Mawr graduates became college instructors becomes more revealing when compared with a 2 percent figure for Wellesley. In addition, while 61 percent of Bryn Mawr women had some graduate school study, only 36 percent of Wellesley graduates did (Table 10).

In order to place these numbers in a more comprehensive perspective, it is useful to compare those of both colleges with those of a coeducational institution. When comparing Wellesley figures to those of the University of Michigan, it is interesting to see that marriage rates for the former are even higher than those for the coeducational college: 58 percent married at Wellesley while 53 percent of University of Michigan women students married (see Appendix, Table 3). Occupation rates are very comparable: 35 percent employment for Wellesley; 34 percent employment for Michigan (see Appendix, Table 2). In addition, advanced study statistics for these two schools show a more marked similarity than either set of figures do when compared with Bryn Mawr. Of Wellesley students, 36 percent had some graduate schooling, while

TABLE 7
Marriage Rates of Wellesley
Graduates

Classes of	1889–93	1894–98	1899–1903	1904–8	Total
Married	52–49%	66–54%	68–49%	150–68%	336–57%
Unmarried	54–51%	56–46%	70–51%	70–32%	250–43%
Total	106	122	138	220	586

Note: based upon a 20 percent sample of Wellesley College graduates taken from Wellesley College Alumnae registers.

TABLE 8
Family Size of Married
Wellesley Graduates

Number of Children Classes of	1889–93	1894–98	1899–1903	1904–8	Total
None	16–31%	18–27%	12–18%	32–21%	78–23%
One	6–12%	20–30%	22–32%	32–21%	80–24%
Two or three	26–50%	16–24%	26–38%	64–43%	132–39%
Four or more	4– 8%	12–18%	8–12%	22–15%	46–14%
Total	52	66	68	150	336

Note: Includes all married Wellesley graduates from Table 7.

21 percent of the University of Michigan women pursued further study (see Appendix, Table 1).

These Michigan statistics give further evidence to the fact that Bryn Mawr did really stand out as a school where, in these years, marriage rates were particularly low and advanced study and occupation rates were quite high. The figures shed light on Wellesley as well. It is interesting that Wellesley students married somewhat more and pursued further study more often than University of Michigan women; these numbers suggest the dual emphasis at Wellesley, where a blend of married life with intellectual pursuits was considered desirable for the model college graduate.

Wellesley College, like many other women's colleges but unlike Bryn Mawr, was first founded in 1870 as a female seminary. As a seminary it sought to combine some intellectual training with explicit domestic objectives which included preparation for household duties. In addition, the student was to acquire "complete and elegant culture" through the

TABLE 9
Occupations of Wellesley Graduates [1,2]

Classes of	1889–93	1894–98	1899–1903	1904–8	Total
Teacher/ tutoring	8– 8%	30–25%	38–28%	32–15%	108–18%
College teaching	8– 8%	2– 2%	–	2– 1%	12– 2%
Clerical work	–	2– 2%	4– 3%	8– 4%	14– 2%
Social work	2– 2%	4– 3%	6– 4%	6– 3%	18– 3%
Librarian	2– 2%	2– 2%	6– 4%	4– 2%	14– 2%
Doctor, lawyer	–	2– 2%	2– 1%	–	4– 2%
Other [3]	4– 4%	8– 7%	6– 4%	16– 7%	34– 6%
None	82–77%	72–59%	76–55%	152–70%	382–65%
Total sample	106	122	138	220	586

[1] based upon a 20 percent sample of Wellesley College graduates taken from Wellesley College alumnae registers.

[2] Occupation listed is one which was pursued for the longest time.

[3] 1889–93 treasurer, actress, writer, farmer; 1894–98 manager of tea room, government worker, authors (2), composer, editors (2), missionary; 1899–1903 copywriter, alumnae trustee, housemother, writer, farmer, store proprietor; 1904–8 fashion coordinator, insurance agent, deaconess, saleslady, bacteriologist, farmers (2), editor, writers (3), storekeepers (2), missionary, housemother.

study of such ornamental subjects as oil painting, drawing, and instrumental music. Henry Durant, the founder of Wellesley, was also particularly interested in the formation of correct, moral habits in his girls, and Bible study was to become a central feature of the program.

The seminary opened as a college in 1875, but its new status did not change its stated purpose. The institution remained essentially an obscure finishing school until Alice Palmer's administration in 1881. Ada L. Howard, the first president, was ineffectual, and the leadership was assumed by Durant, whose lofty ideas of noble, moral womanhood contrasted with his despotic manner. One student wrote of him: "He is as hard as flint and his mind is made up of the most beautiful theories, but he is perfectly blind to facts. He rules the college, from the amount of Latin we shall read to the kind of meat we shall have for dinner; he even went out into the kitchen the other day and told the cook not to waste so much butter in making the hash, for I heard him myself." [16]

Such preoccupation was perhaps not befitting a college administrator. It was not until Alice Freeman Palmer's tenure that the important elements and purposes of Wellesley College life were confronted. She inherited a weak institution out of which she managed to shape a respected college that combined a strong intellectual emphasis with programs designed to cultivate genteel traits and an appreciation of the spiritual joys of domestic life. In trying to develop the woman side and the human side, she created an environment where the so-called "cultural hybrid" could flourish. She hoped that the Wellesley woman would be domesticated yet never mawkish; intelligent and capable of direct action yet never mannish.

Her first priority was to raise the rather meager academic standards. Like Carey Thomas, she made entrance examinations more difficult to attract students of high caliber. The examinations, however, were not as comprehensive as those for Bryn Mawr. She also abolished the preparatory department which had been established for those who were not able to handle college work and was instrumental in founding several independent preparatory schools which would feed qualified students to Wellesley.

The previously confused set of course offerings was standardized and simplified. Students were required to take mathematics and Latin. However, unlike Bryn Mawr students, Wellesley women were not required to take Greek if they preferred to concentrate on the sciences. Moreover, the Wellesley student was allowed more electives whereas the Bryn Mawr student's program was practically all filled with required subjects designed to develop intellectual discipline. Such "frills" as vocal music and drawing were not only offered at Wellesley; they were required subjects. In addition, instrumental music and painting were possible electives.[17]

Alice Freeman Palmer's deep interest in morality, based on Christian tenets, was also reflected in the revised curriculum. To her, one of the greatest gifts that college life could bestow upon students was to instill an enlarged conception of religion that would emphasize a consecrated serving of humanity.[18] Instead of requiring students to attend daily Bible classes—which Wellesley women seemed to consider a chore—Palmer tried to make Bible study more palatable by condensing the time to two hours a week of examinable, serious instruction. Attendance was required at chapel every morning when Alice Freeman would lead the Wellesley community in prayers.[19] Her talks on morality and the importance of serving humanity, which often followed the prayers, contrast with Carey Thomas's morning speeches on the glory of the scholar's life. Each woman used the same opportune time to purvey very different views on goals for educated women.

Palmer also attempted, as did Carey Thomas, to raise the standards of the college by hiring qualified faculty. Alice Freeman Palmer was very much committed to hiring women faculty, and, from the beginning of her administration, women predominated.[20] Carey Thomas would have found some of these women unqualified to teach at Bryn Mawr.

TABLE 10
Advanced Study of
Wellesley Graduates [1,2]

Classes of	1889–93	1894–98	1899–1903	1904–8	Total
Advanced study					
MA	18–17%	12–10%	20–15%	34–15%	84–14%
PhD	4– 4%	4– 3%	2– 1%	—	10– 2%
MD, LLB, or JD	—	6– 5%	2– 1%	—	8– 1%
BS or RN	2– 2%	2– 2%	2– 1%	8– 4%	14– 2%
Advanced study/No degree [3]	16–15%	18–15%	14–10%	46–21%	94–16%
	40–38%	42–34%	40–29%	88–40%	210–36%
No advanced study	66–62%	80–66%	98–71%	132–60%	376–64%
Total sample	106	122	138	220	586

[1] based upon a 20 percent sample of Wellesley College graduates taken from Wellesley College alumnae registers.
[2] In cases where alumnae received two degrees, the more advanced one was recorded.
[3] At least one year.

It was in the area of internal organization of the college that Alice Freeman Palmer really excelled. Her genius for administration and organization was admired by all who knew her. Later in her life, when she had left Wellesley College, she was continually called upon by administrators of schools and various educational programs to advise them about alternative organizational structures. She even traveled to the University of Chicago from Boston for several months out of the years from 1892 to 1895 to serve as Dean of Women and to help organize the emerging women's department. At Wellesley she simplified the formerly complicated college administration. She organized standing committees to formulate policy suggestions on important subjects, such as preparatory schools, entrance examinations, and graduate work. She also founded the Academic Council, consisting of heads of departments,

View of the campus of Wellesley College. Courtesy of Wellesley College Archives.

which she could consult on policy matters. There was less emphasis on departments as isolated units; each department became directly responsible to the president. Alice Freeman, as leader of the college, became the heart of the organization:

> It is impossible for the girls of later days, of more perfect organization and more divided responsibility, to realize how in that early time the whole college depended on this one personality. What she thought and said and did was the centre of what the college thought and said and did. It would have been dangerous for one person to have so much power had not that person been Miss Freeman.[21]

If Bryn Mawr's atmosphere was charged with competitiveness and elitism, the general tenor of Wellesley reflected a subdued, familial grace. Classes at Wellesley were always considerably larger than those at Bryn Mawr; yet the former college sought to provide a feeling of homelike intimacy. A college, in Alice Freeman Palmer's words, should "make for its students a home within its walls." [22] Wellesley women lived in cottages as did Bryn Mawr students, but the rationales for such cozy living quarters differed. At Bryn Mawr the size enabled the influence of academically oriented counselors to be more pervasive; at Wellesley the cottages were seen as conducive to creating a homelike atmosphere. Heads of Wellesley cottages were motherly figures whose role was largely disciplinary, whereas heads of the small Bryn Mawr dormitories were scholars. A rather rigid boarding-school discipline was in effect at Wellesley, whereas at Bryn Mawr students took some part in decision making through the Self Government Association. Although the Association's proposed policies were subject to Carey Thomas's approval, Bryn Mawr women had at least the illusion of sophistication and maturity that Wellesley students lacked.

In addition, Wellesley women were required to aid in some of the lighter domestic work of the college, for, according to the *Wellesley College Circular*, "the discipline of this domestic work, which unites all in one family as helpers for the common good, is invaluable in its influence upon the moral nature in its preparation for social life." [23] While Bryn Mawr students spent their dinners discussing the latest political developments of Tolstoi's new novel, Wellesley women were required to serve their own meals. The manners and taste of Wellesley women were looked after assiduously; students were expected to perform such tasks as hanging pictures, decorating with flowers, and attending concerts. The health of Wellesley students was also carefully overseen, but the

Alice Freeman Palmer. Courtesy of Wellesley College Archives.

A student room at Wellesley College, 1881. Courtesy of Wellesley College Archives.

View of the campus of Bryn Mawr College. Courtesy of Bryn Mawr College Archives.

students practiced individual physical exercises rather than competitive athletics. In a statement that underlies the philosophic differences with Bryn Mawr, a Wellesley dean said: "Fiercely competitive athletics have their dangers for men but they develop manly strength. For women their dangers are greater and the qualities they develop are not womanly." [24]

Alice Freeman Palmer, in committing herself to training women first as women rather than scholars,[25] was concerned with all aspects of her students' development—social, moral, and intellectual. Carey Thomas, on the other hand, saw scholarly prowess as the essential goal of college life. Alice Freeman would consider a student's tardiness in returning from town, lack of personal orderliness, or failure in Latin with equal seriousness. One student described an encounter with her:

> The president was responsible for our going out and coming in. The "office" might give permission to leave town, but all tardiness in returning must be explained to the president. How timidly four of us came to Miss Freeman in my sophomore year to explain that the Freshman's mother had kept us to supper after our "permitted drive on Monday afternoon." What an occasion it gave her to caution us as to sophomore influence over freshmen.[26]

But Wellesley women visited her office with less trepidation than Bryn Mawr students approached the office of Carey Thomas. For, consistent with her own insecurities about her position, Alice Freeman tried to project an image of being head of a great family and frequently referred to the students as "my girls." Although she never lost her dignity and easy power of command, her posture was one of enlightened benevolence.

If Carey Thomas sought to isolate Bryn Mawr students from the social milieu that connected women with domesticity, Alice Freeman wished to expose her students occasionally to Boston society. She tried to cultivate associations within Boston's intelligentsia so that Wellesley women might profit both academically and socially. The Wellesley woman was not trained to lead a life of intellectual renunciation and to seek a sense of solidarity with members of her own sex. Rather, the Wellesley woman, whether married or not, was to use her intelligence and refined tastes to care for those—both male and female—who needed her help and guidance.

But although she was to be part of society, the Wellesley College woman—like her counterpart at Bryn Mawr—had a unique status that set her apart from other women. College-bred women were still a rarity in

M. Carey Thomas. Courtesy of Bryn Mawr College Archives.

Mathematical seminar at Bryn Mawr. Courtesy of the New York Public Library.

late nineteenth-century America; many who graduated in these early years had a sense of being part of an exceptional group. Their feelings of being special often instilled a desire to excel at whatever they pursued—whether it be a career as wife and mother or as college professor. Because many of these women chose not to take the domestic path and marry, their image remained tainted in the eyes of many nineteenth-century Americans, who sometimes went as far as connecting college education to eventual physical deformity for women.

Despite Alice Freeman Palmer's desire to integrate her students into a society that embraced domesticity, many Wellesley women—like Bryn Mawr women—would find it difficult to settle into a life of complacency within a household. Being a "cultural hybrid" could create great conflict in students. At a Wellesley College reunion held in 1887, the toast-mistress went so far as to say that "Not all among us is happy with the peaceful joys of home life." [27] Christopher Lasch has described the so-called neurasthenic woman of the late nineteenth century whose intelligence and extensive education collided with lives of passive consumption: "For women such as these, conscious of their intellectual gifts but unable, it seemed, to make use of them within the sphere of women's traditional duties, life, experiences, 'growth' were always *out there*, they belonged to the great world beyond the household and family." [28]

For some women who graduated in the late nineteenth century, this problem never arose. But for most, their educational experience was fraught with conflict as they tried to fulfill the high moral and academic expectations their college years had instilled. This sense of mission created a comradeship among women college graduates at the end of the nineteenth century; in Carey Thomas's words, there was a feeling of "sex solidarity" among those who had undergone a unique collective experience.

NOTES

1. Mary Wager Fisher, "Bryn Mawr College," *The Home Maker* 8 (September 1892): 420.

2. Martha Carey Thomas, "Notes for the Opening Address at Bryn Mawr College," Bryn Mawr College Archives, 1899.

3. Helen Thomas Flexner, "Bryn Mawr: A Characterisation," *Bryn Mawr Alumnae Quarterly* (January 1908). Helen Thomas Flexner was Carey Thomas's youngest sister; she entered Bryn Mawr College in 1889. According to Edith Finch, the difference in age between the sisters gave Carey Thomas "something of a legendary character" (p. 205) to her sister. Flexner added to the fame of her

older sister by publishing characterizations such as the one cited here. Helen Thomas eventually married Simon Flexner, the first Director of Medical Research at Rockefeller Institute.

4. *Bryn Mawr College Program,* 1895, Bryn Mawr College Archives.

5. Martha Carey Thomas, "The Curriculum of the Women's Colleges—Old Fashioned Disciplines," delivered at the thirty-fourth general meeting of the Association of Collegiate Alumnae and published in the *Journal* of the Association of Collegiate Alumnae 10 (May 1917): 590.

6. Ibid., p. 589.

7. Alvin Johnson, *Pioneer's Progress* (New York, 1952), pp. 138, 145–49. Johnson was kinder to Thomas than most of Bryn Mawr's faculty—particularly the men.

8. *Bryn Mawr College Program,* 1895.

9. Cornelia Meigs, *What Makes a College? A History of Bryn Mawr* (New York, 1956), p. 72. Meigs's portrait of Thomas's administration at Bryn Mawr is far more balanced than that of Edith Finch.

10. Mabel Atkinson, "Bryn Mawr at Play," *Albany Review* [London] 1 (1907): 640–49.

11. Flexner, "Bryn Mawr."

12. Mary Wager Fisher, "Bryn Mawr College," pp. 415–23.

13. All of these figures were compiled from alumnae registers which list information for each graduate. A 20 percent random sample was used, from which the percentages presented were calculated. Statistics were grouped in five-year periods. 1908 was a natural cut-off point because figures for the years 1909–13 generally varied in almost all categories from those for the years 1904–8.

14. The accuracy of the 1910 census has been questioned. However, although 88.6 percent might not be an entirely correct figure, there is a strong sense that the discrepancy between Bryn Mawr students marriage rates and those for the entire country was very great.

15. It should be noted, however, that, unlike other statistical patterns (see note 13), a dramatic increase in marriage rates of Wellesley graduates occurred during the period 1904 to 1908, when 68 percent of the graduates eventually got married as compared with 51 percent for the period from 1889 to 1903. See Table 7.

16. Letter from Elizabeth Stilwell, October 16, 1875 to her mother, quoted in Florence Converse, *The Story of Wellesley* (Boston, 1915), p. 27.

17. Circular for 1876, Wellesley College.

18. Alice Freeman Palmer, "Why Go to College," in *The Teacher: Essays and Addresses on Education* by George Herbert Palmer and Alice Freeman Palmer (Boston, 1908), p. 380.

19. George Herbert Palmer, *Life of Alice Freeman Palmer* (Boston, 1910), p. 145.

20. Converse, p. 76.

21. George Herbert Palmer, *Life,* p. 154.

22. Alice Freeman Palmer, "A Review of the Higher Education for Women," in *Women and the Higher Education,* ed. Anna Brackett (New York, 1893), p. 117.

23. Circular for 1876, Wellesley College.

24. Statement by the Dean of Wellesley College, 1903, reprinted in *Ms.* (July 1973): 64.

25. Mary Emma Wooley, long-time president of Mount Holyoke College, said this of Alice Freeman Palmer in *Alice Freeman Palmer in Memoriam,* Publications of the Association of Collegiate Alumnae (1903).

26. Converse, p. 177. Comments by Mary C. Wiggin, class of 1885.

27. Speech given at the Class Reunion of Wellesley College (Class of 1886) at Norumbega (Cambridge, Mass., 1888), p. 30.

28. Christopher Lasch, *The New Radicalism in America 1889–1963* (New York, 1965), p. 62.

CHAPTER V

The Merging of Collegiate Identity:
Bryn Mawr and Wellesley, 1908-18

In 1900, two years before she died, Alice Freeman Palmer wrote: "The time, too has passed when girls went to college to prepare themselves solely for teaching or for other bread-winning occupations. In considerable numbers they now seek intellectual resources and the enrichment of their private lives." [1] This statement portended the domestic complacency that seemed to characterize women college graduates increasingly after 1910. The fervor with which Carey Thomas attacked traditional feminine priorities and the ambivalences that Wellesley leaders faced in trying to combine intellectual strength with domestic values seemed to fade as the colleges emerged from the period of infancy. Differences in orientation and emphasis between Wellesley and Bryn Mawr were blurred after about 1910; both institutions produced graduates more inclined to marry and less conscious of having a special mission in life as a result of their college experience.

The college experience, however, was no longer unique and no longer provoked the sustained, fierce opposition that it had thirty years before. Many women were passing through colleges and universities, and even Bryn Mawr women did not see a need to prove their aversion to lives of passive indulgence dramatically. Many women, reluctant to denounce domesticity, found the proliferation of career alternatives—mostly in the area of social reform—acceptable. They also welcomed the new scientific

TABLE 11

Comparison of Marriage Rates
for Bryn Mawr Graduates,
1889–1908
and 1909–18

	1889–1908	1909–18	Total
Married	94–47%	92–67%	186–55%
Unmarried	106–53%	46–33%	152–45%
Total	200	138	338

Note: based upon a 20 percent sample of Bryn Mawr graduates taken from the Bryn Mawr alumnae registers.

TABLE 12

Comparison of Marriage Rates
for Wellesley Graduates,
1889–1908 and 1909–18

	1889–1908	1909–18	Total
Married	336–57%	282–72%	618–63%
Unmarried	250–43%	108–27%	358–37%
Total	586	390	976

Note: based upon a 20 percent sample of Wellesley graduates taken from the Wellesley alumnae registers.

TABLE 13

Comparison of Children/No Children
for Married Bryn Mawr Graduates,
1889–1908 and 1909–18

	1889–1908	1909–18	Total
Children	64–68%	68–74%	132–71%
No children	30–32%	24–26%	54–29%
Total	94	92	186

Note: Includes all married Bryn Mawr graduates from 1889–1918 based upon a 20 percent sample.

and technical overtones to discussions about housework and childcare. These careers provided a means of bringing active, professional occupations within the context of traditional femininity, and college women proclaimed their exceptional ability to become society's caretakers. A college education, they claimed, would add a greater executive power, broader interests, and a truer knowledge of the world to the traditional feminine qualities of sympathy, unfailing tenderness, intuition, and high spiritual idealism. Marriage was not considered incompatible with careers; nor was family life itself degraded by women like Carey Thomas who had wished to alter considerably the educated woman's priorities. It is obvious, though, that she failed to do so for a prolonged period even in her own institution. Defiantly different life styles promoted by a college education were by 1910 only sporadically noticeable, for college women clung to domesticity under the guise of sanitary science and domestic hygiene.

Statistics show that more and more Bryn Mawr and Wellesley women were choosing a life in which domestic affairs were the first priority. Of those Bryn Mawr students who graduated in the decade before World War I, 67 percent married as compared with only 47 percent for the period before (see Table 11). Marriage rates for Wellesley women do not show quite the same dramatic increase, yet the figures do change considerably: 57 percent of Wellesley students who graduated between the years 1889 and 1907 married, while 72 percent of those graduating between 1908 and 1918 married (see Table 12).

In addition, more Bryn Mawr and Wellesley women were having children after 1908. Figures for Bryn Mawr indicate that the increase was from 68 to 74 percent (see Table 13). And, while 77 percent of married Wellesley women who graduated between the years 1889 and 1908 had children, 88 percent of those in the later period had children (see Table 14).

Statistics for occupations of Bryn Mawr graduates indicate the percentage of those employed for the first twenty years was an impressive 90 percent; the figure changes to 77 percent after 1908 (see Table 15). Wellesley figures in this category remain almost constant, with 35 percent employed in the first period and 33 percent in the following time period (see Table 16).

Fewer Bryn Mawr women went on to graduate schools after 1908. Of the early graduates, 61 percent had some further study; later, only 49 percent did (see Table 17). For Wellesley students, there is a slight increase. Before 1908, 36 percent attended a graduate school; after that year 43 percent pursued further study (see Table 18).

TABLE 14

Comparison of Children/No Children
for Married Wellesley Graduates,
1889–1908 and 1909–18

	1889–1908	1909–18	Total
Children	258–77%	350–88%	608–83%
No children	78–23%	46–12%	124–17%
Total	336	396	732

Note: Includes all married Wellesley graduates from 1889–
1918 based upon a 20 percent sample.

TABLE 15

Comparison of Occupations
for Bryn Mawr Graduates,
1889–1908
and 1909–18 [1,2]

	1889–1908	1909–18	Total
Teaching/ tutoring	78–39%	32–23%	110–32%
College teaching	20–10%	8– 6%	28– 8%
Clerical Work	17– 8%	18–13%	35–10%
Social work	37–18%	22–16%	59–17%
Librarian	3– 1%	4– 3%	7– 2%
Doctor, lawyer	8– 4%	6– 4%	14– 4%
Other [3]	17– 8%	18–13%	35–10%
None	20–10%	32–23%	52–15%
Total sample	200	140	340

[1] based upon a 20 percent sample of Bryn Mawr college
graduates taken from Bryn Mawr alumnae registers.

[2] Occupation listed was one which was pursued for the
longest time.

[3] 1889–1908, see footnote, 3, Table 8; 1909–18: landscape
architect, writers (4), farmers (3), editors (2), housemothers
(2), statistical worker, lab workers (2), motor corps NLWS,
actress, missionary.

TABLE 16
Comparison of Occupations
for Wellesley Graduates,
1889–1908
and 1909–18 [1,2]

	1889–1908	1909–18	Total
Teaching/			
tutoring	108–18%	74–13%	182–16%
College			
teaching	12– 2%	14– 2%	26– 2%
Clerical work	14– 2%	16– 3%	30– 3%
Social work	18– 3%	22– 4%	40– 3%
Librarian	14– 2%	10– 2%	24– 2%
Doctors,			
lawyers	4– 2%	8– 1%	12– 1%
Other [3]	34– 6%	52– 9%	86– 7%
None	382–65%	390–67%	772–66%
Total sample	586	586	1172

[1] based upon a 20 percent sample of Wellesley College graduates taken from Wellesley College alumnae registers.

[2] Occupation listed is one which was pursued for the longest time.

[3] 1889–1908, see footnote 3, Table 9; 1909–18: hotel manager, assistant chemist, housemothers (4), newspaper workers (2), proprietor service station, editors (5), farmers (5), home demonstrator, photo finisher, research assistants (4), director of public relations, camp director, writers (6), conductor of European tours, business partners (5), housing sociologist, real estate agent, personnel directors (2), composer, actress, salesladies (3), author, storekeepers (3).

By World War I, then, statistics for graduates of these colleges had come to resemble each other more closely. During the late nineteenth century it had seemed that different ways of dealing with domestic values might result in permanently different types of women's colleges. But by 1910, the period of definition that had produced Bryn Mawr's independent woman had passed. The Wellesley woman who might have been torn between marriage and career was now more likely to feel comfortable opting for the domestic life, perhaps trying at certain points to combine it with some kind of occupation.

Interestingly, the statistics for both of these colleges now not only resembled each other but also approached the pattern of the University

TABLE 17
Comparison of Advanced Study
for Bryn Mawr Graduates,
1889-1908
and 1909-18 [1],[2]

	1889-1908	1909-18	Total
Advanced study			
MA	29–14%	28–20%	57–17%
PhD	9– 4%	6– 4%	15– 4%
MD, LLB, or JD	8– 4%	6– 4%	14– 4%
Advanced study/No degree [3]	76–38%	28–20%	104–31%
Subtotal	122–61%	68–49%	190–56%
No advanced study	78–39%	72–51%	150–44%
Total sample	200	140	340

[1] based upon a 20 percent sample of Bryn Mawr college graduates taken from Bryn Mawr college alumnae registers.

[2] In cases where alumnae received two degrees, the more advanced one was recorded.

[3] At least one year.

of Michigan. It is very important to point out, though, that statistics for Michigan for the years 1909-18 are not entirely accurate because the alumnae register for early graduates was published in 1925. Thus, marriage and advanced study rates must surely have been higher, while occupational statistics are probably fairly accurate. However, despite the probable inaccuracies, it seems evident that statistics for the University of Michigan did not change as much as those for Bryn Mawr—and possibly Wellesley as well—over the period of approximately thirty years (1889-1918) (see Appendix, Tables 4, 5, and 6). University of Michigan women students were more apt to marry and at least slightly more apt to pursue advanced study in the later period, but occupational rates remained the same. The pattern is similar to that of Wellesley College, although Wellesley students probably still showed more of a tendency to marry, and, almost certainly, to attend graduate school than did University of Michigan women. The figures for Michigan are significant,

TABLE 18
Comparison of Advanced Study
for Wellesley Graduates,
1889–1908
and 1909–18 [1],[2]

	1889–1908	1909–18	Total
Advanced Study			
MA	84–14%	114–19%	198–17%
PhD	10– 2%	14– 2%	24– 2%
MD, LLB, or JD	8– 1%	10– 2%	18– 2%
BS or RN	14– 2%	34– 6%	48– 4%
Advanced study/No degree [3]	94–16%	80–14%	174–15%
Subtotal	210–36%	252–43%	462–39%
No advanced study	376–64%	334–57%	710–61%
Total sample	586	586	1172

[1] based upon a 20 percent sample of Wellesley College graduates taken from Wellesley College registers.

[2] In cases where alumnae received two degrees, the more advanced one was recorded.

[3] At least one year.

for they confirm that the women's colleges were not only becoming more alike by 1910, but were coming to resemble coeducational institutions as well. The attempt to create separate colleges where women might transmit their own values and where these values might influence the graduates was becoming increasingly ineffective.

At Bryn Mawr differences between the earlier and later periods were naturally more acute, for Carey Thomas never conceived of the college as oriented toward preserving domestic values. But more and more, after 1910, Carey Thomas's viewpoints did not dictate policy at Bryn Mawr. Indeed, the most significant changes at the college began to occur as Carey Thomas became less of an autocrat; she became less mythlike and regal, more human and frail. No longer were Carey Thomas and Bryn Mawr inextricably linked:

And it was perhaps inevitable that she should be blind . . . to the fact that the College was growing up, with more and more of its own capacity for advancement and development. It had been an entity of its own even when it came into her hands; it was even more so now—Carey Thomas was not the College, nor was the College Carey Thomas, no matter what the outside world might think. It was conceivable that the College might outgrow her and ride over her.[2]

Alvin Johnson, an early member of Bryn Mawr's faculty, wrote of Thomas: "With so imperial a head as President Thomas, the presumptions a college granted might be cancelled or prorogued."[3] Carey Thomas had a rather notorious reputation among college professors all over the country for hiring and firing people at will and for allowing faculty members almost no control over any area of college life—or even of their own lives. Rules were handed down by President Thomas that the faculty could never challenge. For example, professors at Bryn Mawr were denied the right to lecture outside of the college, had to teach during summer sessions, and were required to attend commencement. But after 1910 the shifting of power away from centralized administrations to pockets of authority throughout university faculties began to penetrate even Bryn Mawr. Carey Thomas relinquished some of her power, but she did so only after a struggle with the faculty, which came to a head in 1916. The incident that finally brought on the crisis at Bryn Mawr concerned a Professor Richard Holbrook of the Italian department, who applied for a promotion to full professor. Thomas turned down the request, saying that the Italian department was of "insufficient" importance to merit a full professor. Furthermore, she told him that his employment would be concluded if he did not remain an associate professor. The case might have ended here, as did so many others, except that the *Public Ledger* in Philadelphia took up Holbrook's cause and printed an article extremely critical of President Thomas. She protested vehemently, threatening to sue the newspaper for defamation of character. Months of publicity and turmoil followed the incident, during which time Bryn Mawr's full professors drew up a plan for a faculty government excluding President Thomas.

The revolt finally ended and Bryn Mawr was spared further publicity. But the college had changed during that time; Thomas was no longer the sole administrative force. She submitted to a plan of government that gave faculty members authority over such critical matters as promotion and appointments. Although Carey Thomas would never publicly discuss her feelings about the incident, it is clear that she began to see the trends of the time lessening her control of Bryn Mawr. And as outside pressures started to seep into the college that Thomas had tried so hard to isolate, she, too, began to seek outside preoccupations to soothe the strains of her surrenders to new necessities.[4]

Her relations with students underwent comparable changes. Nine-teenth-century students had shown real devotion to her; many were even in awe of her majestic presence. But by 1910 admiration was tinged with criticism, and students tried to modify her harsh directives. The Self Government Association began to become a real vehicle for change when student leaders finally succeeded in regulating the cut rule and in allowing weekend absences. Carey Thomas characteristically did not give in easily. Interspersed among grandiose speeches urging Bryn Mawr women to serve humanity were biting lectures in which she decried the declining standards of the college, and tried to defend the necessity of strictly regulated attendance and weekend passes.[5]

The curriculum and entrance requirements were affected by the decline of Carey Thomas's omnipotence at Bryn Mawr. Both faculty and students combined forces to modify the dreaded senior oral examina-tions. The faculty succeeded in allowing entering students to take a choice of examinations rather than the standard test given by Bryn Mawr. In addition, more electives were offered and Greek—the symbol of a classical curriculum—was no longer required. Among the electives were courses in such practical subjects as pedagogy, previously anath-ema to Carey Thomas. There were some subjects, however, such as music and home economics, which never were given a place in Bryn Mawr's program.

But students clamored for these subjects. It was becoming clear that most Bryn Mawr women who entered after about 1910 were less interested in classical Greek than they were in childcare and home economy. One student wrote: "As Miss Thomas always told us when we complained about having no courses on babies or music, 'when you want information go to the experts. We can not give you the best here, and we will not give you anything else.' " [6] Statistics confirm an early trend away from classical disciplinary studies toward more modern subjects such as English literature and romance languages. During the years 1889 to 1893, for example, 30 percent of Bryn Mawr graduates majored in classical languages. In a later period—1908 to 1918—only 9 percent concentrated in this area. There were also more science majors and fewer students interested in philosophy.

There was one area of professional study, however, that Carey Thomas had previously dismissed as completely unsuitable in a liberal arts curriculum, which she now embraced almost passionately. As was mentioned previously, she began about 1910 to accept courses in social work and urged her students to involve themselves wholeheartedly in social problems with almost the same degree of fervor that she had once urged women to lead lives of scholarly detachment. It was the one major concession that she voluntarily made to the changing times, and she was aware of it: "On other subjects I have reversed my earlier opinions as the result of later experiences and have become truly radical. On social questions, for example, I find from discussions with our Bryn Mawr seniors at my 'at homes' that I am even ahead of the most progressive of them." [7] In 1916 the Carola Woerishoffer School of Social Economy and Social Research was founded; it was primarily a graduate school, although Bryn Mawr undergraduates could take courses. M. Carey Thomas was proud of its eventual success, and always saw it in part as a monument to her ability to adapt to the times.

By 1916, then, Bryn Mawr was no longer an impenetrable fortress where intellectual discipline took absolute priority. Instead, academic standards were loosened, professional courses were introduced, and graduates displayed more of a propensity to marry and raise families. Carey Thomas, who had less responsibility for running the college, spent more of her time working in the suffrage and peace movements, and, with the advent of World War I, plunged Bryn Mawr into a flurry of work to help the war effort. In 1919 and 1920 her growing detachment from Bryn Mawr was evident when she took an unprecedented leave of absence in order to travel around the world. When she returned, much of her effort was concentrated in creating at Bryn Mawr a Summer School for Working Women, which opened in 1921. The school and its students were—perhaps more than anything else—symbols of Bryn Mawr's evolution from an isolated scholarship-oriented community to an involved, socially concerned one.

At Wellesley, always less extreme, changes were not as pronounced. During the nineteenth century, life at Wellesley combined some challenging intellectual study with an abundance of programs designed to teach students domestic amenities. But as the twentieth century progressed, the balance changed slightly with more emphasis being placed on competitive academics and somewhat less on domestic work and boarding-school discipline. Statistics for Wellesley show that, while more students were marrying and having children in the period from 1908 to 1918 than in the previous twenty years, there was also a slight increase in the number of graduates who pursued further study and those who had some kind of occupation. The increased emphasis on academia at Wellesley and the diminution of the elitism and untouchable intellectual standards at Bryn Mawr enabled some blurring of differences between the two colleges to occur.

In 1896 the Wellesley requirement that students participate in the domestic work of the college was ended. Along with the discontinuation of this obligation, Wellesley women were given more of an opportunity to make their own decisions about some aspects of their college life. A Self Government Association was formed after Alice Palmer's presidency which lobbied successfully for—among other things—the removal of the ban on theater and opera at Wellesley and the permission for seniors to leave the college at their own discretion.[8]

Courses in such areas as pedagogy and music had always been part of Wellesley's curriculum. Additions were made later, particularly in the area of social economy. During the late 1880s Katherine Cowan, an activist who was to help found the College Settlement Association, gave courses at Wellesley. But along with these professionalized courses, the whole curriculum was made stronger, and students were encouraged to compete with one another. Until 1897, students at Wellesley were never told about grades, as it was feared that excessively competitive, and therefore unfemininine, behavior would ensue.[9]

By 1891 attendance at Bible classes and prayer sessions was made optional. However, the abolition of compulsory religion did not in any way squelch the social impulse so evident at Wellesley. In a context divorced from religious implication, moral fervor and a desire to serve humanity were still characteristic of much of the Wellesley community. In 1891, the same year that compulsory prayers were abolished, the College Settlement Association opened a branch at Wellesley College, giving Wellesley women an opportunity to satisfy their service impulse as well as their sense of mission. Some Wellesley students continued to work and live in settlements after graduation. John Rousmanière has stated that the settlement house provided them with an opportunity to support their vulnerable status as "cultural hybrids" so that they might regain the equilibrium they had been secure in at college.[10] Bryn Mawr women were never as active in settlement work, partially because social concern was not a popular theme on the campus until after 1910. Also, Thomas did not like to conceive of social work as a feminine-dominated occupation, and settlement houses were often made up almost solely of women.

There were certain administrative changes at Wellesley which seemed to correspond to those at Bryn Mawr, although at Wellesley the transitions were easier. During Alice Freeman Palmer's tenure, she had many diverse responsibilities and roles and her office was the one real center of power. She did not apportion her duties to assistants. Professor Whiting of Wellesley said of her: "I think of her in her office . . . with not even a skilled secretary at first, toiling with all the correspondence, seeing individual girls on academic and social matters, setting them right in cases of discipline, interviewing members of the faculty on necessary plans." [11] She took care of all disciplinary matters as well as issues concerning academia. But by Caroline Hazard's tenure, from 1899 to 1911, responsibilities were much more diffused. The faculty was more involved in policy decisions; a dean was hired who handled strictly academic work, leaving the president free to supervise the external relations of the college and home administration.[12] At Bryn Mawr, Carey Thomas's long tenure and her own identification with the life of the college combined to make her reluctant to relinquish authority. Thus, the transition to a less centrally controlled administration was fraught with bitterness.

Despite Wellesley's concessions to a strengthened academic program, images of wives and mothers sacrificing their lives for the good of humanity remained very much alive at the college. As was previously stated, by 1910 more Wellesley graduates were marrying and having children than ever before. In 1904, Caroline Hazard, then president of Wellesley College, made a speech exalting the spirit of motherhood, echoing talks by Alice Freeman Palmer given twenty years before: "Whether we recognize it or not, we are the mothers of men. Even those women who have no actual children have children of their spirits. The maternal power of love and sacrifice is our greatest glory. To develop that capacity by pure thought, by right living, by self-control, by humility, and by prayer, this is our first duty, not only for ourselves, but for all whom we love." [13]

It is apparent, then, that after several generations of college women had graduated, neither Bryn Mawr—which had seemed so radically unlike educational institutions for women—nor Wellesley were producing militantly sexless Amazons. Nor did these institutions represent any radical departures from some of the most intellectually rigorous academies and seminaries which abounded in the nineteenth century. While colleges for women may have offered more of a sophisticated academic training, they did not permanently challenge the domesticity cult, prescribing a role of subservience and dedication to the home and family for women.

NOTES

1. Alice Freeman Palmer, "Women's Education in the Nineteenth Century," which appeared in the *New York Evening Post* in 1900 and was reprinted in *The Teacher: Essays and Addresses on Education* by George Herbert Palmer and Alice Freeman Palmer (Boston, 1908), p. 350.

2. Cornelia Meigs, *What Makes a College? A History of Bryn Mawr* (New York, 1956), p. 99.

3. Alvin Johnson, *Pioneer's Progress* (New York, 1952), p. 149.

4. Meigs, pp. 93-99.

5. Martha Carey Thomas, "The Regulation of Attendance at Bryn Mawr College in the Year 1914–15," in the *Bryn Mawr Alumnae Quarterly* 8 (January 1915), Bryn Mawr College Archives.

6. Bulletins—Class of 1916, statement by Isabel Vincent Harper.

7. Martha Carey Thomas, "The Curriculum of the Women's Colleges—Old Fashioned Disciplines," delivered at the thirty-fourth general meeting of the Association of Collegiate Alumnae and published in the *Journal of the Association of Collegiate Alumnae* 10 (May 1917): 588.

8. Florence Converse, *The Story of Wellesley* (Boston, 1915).

9. Ibid.

10. John P. Rousmanière, "Cultural Hybrid in the Slums: The College Woman and the Settlement House, 1889–94," in *Education in American History—Readings on the Social Issues,* ed. Michael Katz (New York, 1973), pp. 122–238.

11. Converse, p. 72.

12. Ibid., p. 104.

13. Caroline Hazard, "A Woman's Influence," address given at Park Street Church, Boston, October 26, 1904, reprinted in *From College Gates* (Boston, 1925), pp. 144–45.

CHAPTER VI

The Association of Collegiate Alumnae, 1881-1918

The broader implications of the change that occurred so dramatically at Bryn Mawr and to a lesser extent at Wellesley can be understood by studying the Association of Collegiate Alumnae, later known as the American Association of University Women during the years from its founding in 1881 to the First World War. It was within the ACA arena that women from these two colleges as well as most other colleges attended by women discussed and evaluated their academic experiences and tried to find ways of solving the problems inherent in the confrontation between higher education and domesticity. Graduates attending the annual and regional conferences who still had affiliations with colleges went back to their schools filled with ideas about possible roles for college women and necessary curriculum changes for achieving new goals. The American Association of University Women in its early years had a more pervasive influence than it has now; college women then constituted a small group, convinced of their special status yet insecure about their place within a society that did not fully accept them. Therefore, the ACA served an important function, for it was here that they eventually sought to define careers for themselves that would satisfy needs to be special as well as needs to conform. On a more basic level, they sought companionship with those who lived through a common uniting experience. Estranged from each other, many of these women felt lonely: " 'It came to me,' said a New Hampshire girl who had just graduated and was teaching in Omaha, 'and I joined. I felt as if I had been flung out into space, and the notices of these meetings were the only threads that connected me with the things I had known.' " [1]

This New Hampshire girl, like so many first-generation college women, dreaded caricatures of educated women as asexual and physically grotesque. These first college women were acutely aware that many Americans expected them to appear in "hoofs and horns," and they deplored such stereotypes unanimously. Yet most ACA women did not actively seek to combat the distrust that surrounded them for several reasons. First, they came to the ACA primarily from the infant New England women's colleges where their isolation heightened notions of their special status. A strong feeling of comradery developed, nourished by the scholarly ideal and the hostility of those who thought such ideals inappropriate for women. Second, and perhaps more important, socially acceptable avenues did not yet exist other than teaching and perhaps a few other fields such as nursing where women might have had opportunities for assimilation. Thus, the early ACA membership stayed close to its own academic circles. Occasionally, a figure such as M. Carey Thomas would respond angrily to comments about women's unsuitability for college, but most women preferred to uphold their scholarly excellence within the confines of the ACA and their own institutions.

For first-generation college women, achievement was defined primarily in scholarly terms: they could prove themselves the intellectual equals of men and still remain in relative isolation. In the 1880s no strong model for college women emerged other than the academic. And although not all of the ACA membership subscribed to it equally fervently, the image persisted for lack of any other. When Bryn Mawr opened in 1885, it was welcomed by the ACA for its high standards and commitment to rigorous scholarship. Helen Hiscock Backus, an early president of the ACA, called it a "potent and constant" influence which should serve as a model institution for women.[2] The feasibility of aiding students in pursuing postgraduate study and eventually a college teaching career was one of the first subjects investigated by the ACA. The association offered fellowships for graduate work, and tried to encourage students to study abroad, for some of the European universities were considered the most prestigious.

In its early years the ACA kept aloof from any outside associations—shunning even women's organizations—by virtue of its special educational status. Attempts to communicate with the outside world were largely indirect and rather passive. The ACA did make some attempt to combat the stereotypes concerning women's alleged inability to perform in academia because of physical weakness. It sponsored a research project in the 1880s on the subject of health and physical education of college women. Edward H. Clarke's book *Sex in Education,* which proclaimed that the pressures of scholarship would damage a woman's health, had been a sensational bestseller in the 1870s. It had sparked a whole series of "scientific" articles on the subject in the 1870s and 1880s in such journals as the *American Journal of Heredity* and the *Popular Science Monthly.*[3] The ACA study questioned 705 students, and discovered that 60 percent experienced no change in health, 20 percent had a slight deterioration, and 20 percent reported that they were in better health at the end of their college years. Furthermore, the ACA discovered that the trend of the student's health went back to childhood and had little, if anything, to do with their college experience.[4]

Aside from such published reports, the ACA membership did not seem eager for excessive communication with outsiders. No guest speakers came to their conventions or meetings. The isolation of their college years seemed to be reinforced in their association. Emphasis upon scholarship as the area in which they would affirm their special status did not lend itself to social interaction with the outside world. And, given the hostility toward educated women, it was no wonder that they felt a need to shelter themselves.

The widespread hostility toward a college education for women was supported largely by fears about women's loss of physical as well as behavioral femininity. This general view was ignited and sustained by men in academia like Edward Clarke, professor at Harvard Medical School. Popular magazines such as *Outlook, Arena, Century,* and the *North American Review* carried articles which, if critical, were generally mildly written and had more to say about the content than the form of women's education. Often the authors were women.[5] The articulate specific arguments came from some university men like Charles Eliot, whose position alone gave tremendous weight to his statements. The sensationalism of Clarke and "scientists" writing in the *Popular Science Monthly* abated by the late 1880s—perhaps when it was becoming clear that higher education for women would survive despite the inflammatory tracts and that women were not turning into Amazons. But this did not mean the eventual end of opposition, particularly from university men. In the early 1900s coeducation was flourishing; women outnumbered men in some institutions and threatened to do so in others (see Table 19). Women's encroachment upon institutions run by men coincided with the publication of G. Stanley Hall's *Adolescence* in 1904, which surveyed the literature hostile to women's higher education and denounced women's quest for equal education. The result would be, he wrote, women who are:

> functionally castrated; some actively deplore the necessity of child-bearing, and perhaps are parturition phobiacs, and abhor the limitations of married life; they are incensed whenever attention is called to the functions peculiar to their sex, and the careful consideration of problems of the monthly rest are thought "not fit for cultivated women." [6]

TABLE 19
Comparison of Women and Men
Graduates for the University of Michigan,
1872–1918
(in percent)

	Women	Men
1872–88	17	83
1889–93	33	67
1894–98	40	60
1899–1903	47	53
1904–8	48	52
1909–13	41	59
1914–18	41	59

Note: based on the total population of University of Michigan graduates taken from the University of Michigan alumni registers.

Hall's chapter on women spurred a whole new series of articles, similar to those published after Clarke, about "race suicide," [7] but the reaction was not, as will be seen, to cut off access to education. Rather, the trend was to try to contain the enrollment of women in coeducational institutions (see Table 19—particularly the change from 1904/8 to 1909/13) and, in some cases, to segregate women in separate classes within the larger university.[8] Also, a real effort was made, primarily by university men, to change the focus of women's curricula in coeducational as well as women's colleges and make them more attuned to the needs of a domestic life. The effort came at the same time that specialized courses in such fields as engineering and commerce were being offered in the larger universities on the undergraduate level; by 1900 "professional utility" was considered "a valid reason for undergraduate study of a subject."[9] Thus, it seemed only logical for women to study home economy: it would satisfy demands of domestic ideology as well as new university arrangements. And by the 1890s women, many of whom were now graduating from midwestern and farwestern coeducational institutions where college years did not engender a sense of isolation, were increasingly open to discussing possibilities of using their college education to increase their domestic talents rather than to detract from them.

Therefore, the mere access to education did not alter the consciousness of these first-generation college women in the same ways. Not all women would feel comfortable with the image of themselves as committed solely to scholarship. Their united front withered with the gradual acceptance of a woman's right to go to college and the undermining of the exaggerated ideas about the damage that a college education would inflict on a woman. Coeducation was drawing attention away from those small New England colleges especially suspect of breeding anomalies. Martha Carey Thomas and Alice Freeman Palmer, both active members of the ACA, could agree on the desirability of a college education for talented women and could both deplore the statements of such opponents as Dr. Clarke. Yet they had quite different ideas about the type who would ideally emerge from the academic environment. By the early 1890s this lack of homogeneity became apparent. The unity fostered by the founders' sense of uniqueness as well as their need to prove women's scholarly competence gave way to some diversity of opinion about college curricula and future occupations for college women.

M. Carey Thomas, who consistently gave speeches calling for curricula untainted by modifications preparing women for a home and family, was joined in her plea for pure scholarship by several women—notably Abby Leach, professor of classics at Vassar—who believed that questions of wifehood and motherhood were out of place in a college course, and that a college training should not differ for men and women. Leach said: "Really, I should feel that the 'female college,' which has but lately been ousted from our terminology, had returned in full force if chemistry and physiology and biology were to be taught merely to subserve the ends of the household."[10] Women with the views of Thomas and Leach were outnumbered in the ACA, though. Admiration for Bryn Mawr College was becoming muted, for most women now sought a way to reconcile intellectuality with womanliness, which meant most often wifehood and motherhood. Professor Mary Roberts Smith of Stanford expressed an opinion consistent with traditionally held beliefs about the sanctity of domestic life when she said that "the possibility of motherhood is the primary consideration to which the aims of self-culture and self-support must forever be subordinated." [11]

It was becoming clear that most college-educated women would not—and should not—become scholars. The increasing number of college women after 1890 no longer felt a need to justify their own existences as well as their own careers in academic terms. But nor was it desirable that they all hibernate in homes, with only their college textbooks to remind them of their intellectual training. What, then, should be the fate of the college woman? This question preoccupied ACA members in the last decade of the nineteenth century. Articles and speeches written by ACA constituents asked over and over again which occupations would best be suited to college women. From the responses it is apparent that most women were sensitive to the need to bring traditional womanhood and their intellectual training together. Pressures from nineteenth-century society to have women conform to images of subservient females coincided with these women's own desires to seek appropriately serving roles for themselves—a desire fostered, of course, by their own contact with society. The ACA became a forum for the discussion of possible careers and, thus, the association helped to define and legitimize specific occupations.

Significantly, the search for careers came when industrialization, immigration, and urbanization were descending in full force upon American society. A large part of the urban population became dependent, needing not only employment but also help in coping with the traumatic and often alien urban environment. The concept of a professional corps of social service workers arose; it largely was up to women to supply the personnel. And because of the joining of scientific advances with service occupations, covering everything from domestic science to sanitary science to the legitimization of social service work through psychology and sociology, such occupations became particularly appealing to college women. They could justify their training because of its usefulness to society, and, no less important, because of its kinship with traditional women's work.[12]

It took time for ACA women to opt for such well-defined careers. Women making speeches before the ACA in the late 1880s and 1890s had difficulty precisely defining possible careers for the membership. Teaching was always a possibility, but it was a possibility before women's colleges and did not carry with it an aura of special status; in addition, there was overcrowding in the field and finding a job was not always easy, even with a college diploma. In 1896 Kate Holladay Claghorn, who two years later became secretary-treasurer of the ACA and its first paid employee, gave a speech in which she said that nine out of ten women college graduates who worked in paid occupations went into teaching. Women fear risks and publicity, she said, and teaching was a comfortable occupation.[13] In the same year an effort was made to enumerate possible occupations through the publication of a survey using material supplied by the Massachusetts Bureau of Labor Statistics. Entitled "Compensation in Certain Occupations of Women Who Have Received College or Other Special Training," the list was not very enlightening, for the occupations seemed rather traditional and ordinary: teachers, librarians, stenographers, nurses and supervisors of nursing, journalists, and clerks.[14]

The thrust toward bringing social work careers into a position once occupied by scholarly pursuits began in the ACA in 1887 with the publication of a series of speeches, presented at the national convention, on the opportunities for college women in philanthropic work. The articles condemned so-called "fashionable" charities, and urged the educated woman to search for people truly in need of her services. She should use her "moral and mental power" to further the "elevation of the race."[15] College administrators were urged to give their students preparation for philanthropical work. Such statements were vague, yet they portended the immense interest that college women would come to have in the subject of philanthropy. The term "philanthropical" would be changed to "social"—altering connotations of pure volunteerism—and scientific knowledge would be brought to the field, making these careers appear more professional.

A common theme in articles and speeches urging women to pursue social work was the notion that this career offered a unique opportunity for college women to unite womanliness with intellectuality. Social work was an area in which the eternal feminine qualities—sympathy, tenderness, intuition, and high spiritual ideals—might combine with the broader interests and truer knowledge of the world which a college education provided.[16] Other careers, too, might easily combine these two facets of a college woman, and they were given some attention. Most notable was the field of child psychology, not so far removed from social work. Miss Millicent W. Shinn headed an ACA subcommittee on child study, and she urged women to study in "a field at once so fascinating to womanly instinct and so promising to intellectual ambition."[17] If a woman did not become a professional child psychologist, at least she would have the satisfaction of studying her own child. Ellen H. Richards, more than any other woman in the ACA, echoed the theme of union between womanliness and intellectuality through social work. Her background in chemistry and her interest in efficiency in the home

Ellen Swallow Richards. Courtesy of the New York Public Library.

George Herbert Palmer. Courtesy of Wellesley College Archives.

combined to make her a strong advocate for careers in applied science for women. As early as 1890 she discussed the need for college women in domestic science and sanitary science. "We have been told of our mental ability...," she said. "But the kind of influence we should have on the source of political economy—the kitchen—has been ignored." [18] The kitchen no longer was seen as a mundane place where a woman performed her drudgery; rather, it was seen by Richards and an increasing number of ACA members as the bedrock of the nation's economy. Surely domestic science would dignify a woman's true sphere. Richards used her committee on euthenics, which was concerned with seeking ways to improve the human condition through the betterment of living conditions in kitchens, streets, and public schools, as a forum to convince college women to seek careers in hygiene, in domestic economy, and in sanitary science.

The fact that Ellen Richards and her committee as well as other ACA members were concerned with improving conditions in the public schools is indicative of the larger dimensions that the urban schools began to acquire for socially conscious college women. No longer was the school merely a place to teach; it was also the focus of social work operations. The buildings themselves were often found to be unsanitary and poorly ventilated; food was ill-prepared and not nutritious. Children from immigrant homes or from impoverished surroundings needed attention paid to basic needs as well as to arithmetic and spelling. In articles in ACA publications, "practical problems" associated with public schools—such as hygiene, fire, light, and ventilation—were stressed. Public school improvement brought the ACA into working contact with other organizations that they had formerly shunned. In 1898 Annie Howes Barus, a very active ACA member who had compiled the study on health statistics, made a speech before the association in which she noted that the National Federation of Women's Clubs was active in trying to improve conditions in the public school systems. Here was an area of concern to both groups, she said, and she urged the association to work with the federation. Although the ACA had voted against a resolution three years before to join the National Council for Women, of which the Federation of Women's Clubs was a member, they agreed in 1898 to cooperate with women's clubs on issues involving the welfare of public school children.[19] Similarly, the ACA and the National Education Association, which had had a history of nonaffiliation, came together over this issue.[20] In 1907 the ACA agreed, along with representatives for women's clubs, to form the School Patrons Department of the NEA, which was charged with bringing the home and school closer together.

By the beginning of the twentieth century, the ACA membership seemed less concerned with proving physical and mental ability to withstand college and with isolating themselves because of their special status. Indeed, the shift from a concentration on individual growth to community action was dramatic. "Mere culture" underwent a severe decline. In a questionnaire given to ACA members in 1910 about the aims of higher education for women, the following conclusions were reported: "Higher education of women should adapt itself to meet the new trend in education and living which aims at the well-being of the race rather than at mere culture alone; at the efficiency of the individual as a member of society as well as a skilled worker in a chosen profession or trade." [21] The catchwords of the day had changed from culture and academics to profession and efficiency.

The ideal was no longer to live one's life in scholarly solitude; rather, one should strive to help people to make the most of the resources available to them, to use new scientific advances in order to promote health and well-being and combat urban squalor. In an article entitled "Economic Efficiency of the College Woman," Susan M. Kingsbury, who taught economics at Simmons, the new technical college for women, wrote that the college woman must be trained for business sense, particularly in the area of the "economics of consumption." Manual skills formerly learned in the home were no longer useful; the home had changed from a center of production to one of consumption, and educated women had to be schooled in the "economics of consumption." She, in turn, would pass on her skills and knowledge to others.[22] A description of Ellen Richard's committee on euthenics broadens considerably the ideas of profession and efficiency: "Her program was indeed an ambitious one, for it embraced education of the public 'to esteem better environment,' to arouse people 'to the waste of life and the possible saving,' to the need of child study and care, to the necessity of medical inspection in schools, to the relationship between employer and employee, and to better budgeting 'of income and expenditure by the salaried class.'" [23]

By 1910, the ACA presented a socially conscious image. The members were also, by and large, intensely aware of the distinctiveness of femininity; the joining of professional commitment with traditional female concerns in these new careers was satisfying to college women who were averse to rejecting all domestic values. But the explanation for the change in orientation lies only partially in the women themselves. It is clear that the outside world, particularly men in education and government, was not only accepting these new careers, but was actually praising higher education for leading college women to them. Here were acceptable outlets for women's excessive education. More than that, though, political uses might be made of women's aspirations: women might serve a role in helping to alleviate some of the destruction wrought by rapid industrialization. If indeed women began to redefine the "home" in a much broader sense, they might help to bolster deteriorating conditions in the streets, in the schools, in the factories. The bad effects of urbanization and industrialization might be brought under control. Sanitary science could alleviate urban discontentment, and thus could be flaunted by those particularly committed to the status quo. As social workers themselves, women would *contribute* to the attempt to control urban chaos but never to shape or reinterpret values worth saving. They were ushered into social service only *after* "science" had made the work primarily technical. However, women were really caught in the middle because they themselves were, if not being "controlled," certainly encouraged by men who saw social service work as suitable for the overambitious (not the intellectual) woman.

Perhaps nothing is so illustrative of this outside support as the parade of distinguished men—primarily academics—who came to speak before the ACA and who began to write articles for ACA publications after 1900. They did not offer financial support (the ACA supported itself in these years through membership dues),[24] but they did bring satisfaction to many ACA members who saw favorable public opinion as vital to their careers. Some of these men, such as Charles Eliot, had previously been hostile to college-educated women; thus their presence was even more of an indication that educated women had become socially acceptable. The first of these visitors were William Harper, president of the University of Chicago, and Benjamin Andrews, superintendent of schools in Chicago, who gave addresses of welcome at the February 1900 annual meeting of the ACA in Chicago. The theme was public schools as a desirable place for college women to work as teachers and as social workers. Harper spoke of the sensitive, careful nature of elementary school teaching and women's natural fitness for it: "In my opinion the greatest career in life for a woman, next to that of mother, is that of teacher. . . ." [25] Harper's comment about motherhood did not seem to disturb the assembly of women; according to the minutes, they reacted warmly to his remarks. During his speech, Harper must surely have been aware that at the University of Chicago the enrollment of women was threatening to exceed that of men; in 1902, he advocated the segregation of sexes at the University of Chicago in order that women might receive adequate preparation for their lives as mothers and teachers! [26]

In 1903 the meeting was held in Washington, D.C., and a keynote speaker was Professor William Henry Lefavour.[27] He talked of the trend toward utilitarianism and specialization in men's education, and noted that this trend should be adopted in women's education—not for preparation in such fields as law, medicine, theology, and pure scientific research but for preparation in the laws and economy of the home. He went on to list six other possible lines of work for women aside from teaching: institutional housekeeping (perhaps in a social settlement), stenography and typing, nursing, library work, arts and crafts (pottery or bookbinding), and landscape gardening (and maybe *even* landscape architecture). Lefavour spoke of using the principle of specialization to legitimize offering subjects that would appeal to women.[28] It is apparent that university men saw the reverse as also true: the specialized courses for women would help to legitimize a whole host of specialized courses for men as well. This speech was insulting to intellectually oriented women, but no rebuttal ever was given. Indeed, the opening address of the 1903 meeting, given by the president of the Washington branch, was only redundant. She said: "If we have an outlook that extends a little beyond the household, we must not neglect the properly conducted home." [29]

A year later, in 1904, G. Stanley Hall's *Adolescence* was published. College women's reaction to Hall was muted; the weak defense indicated that many women had already made scholarship subservient to traditional feminine occupations. May Cheney, an active member of the ACA, responded to Hall by challenging his marital statistics on college women. However, she went on to say that "the strongest argument in favor of educating women is that it prepares them to be wiser and better mothers. If our present system of education leads to sterility, it is our duty to find a different system which shall not operate to cut off the most enterprising and highly developed class of society." [30]

Hall's statements did not discourage the continued support of the ACA given by influential outsiders. Indeed, they only encouraged further explication of notions of professionalism and efficiency as applied to the home and the extended home. Professor Charles Richman Henderson, chaplain of the University of Chicago, talked to the ACA membership about the desirability of professional social service training; courses would involve technical practice as well as theory.[31] Professor Edward T. Devine of the University of Pennsylvania spoke of the necessity for women to remain wage spenders instead of wage earners and to be educated as such. This arrangement, he said, did not violate the economic independence of women: "I would not admit that the family as at present constituted, with a wage-earning male head and a wage-spending female head, is incompatible with the entire economic independence of women." Devine also spoke of the fact that he must take his place as a conservative scorned by Charlotte Perkins Gilman,[32] a writer and feminist. Significantly, Charlotte Gilman never spoke before the ACA or wrote an article for their publications refuting such statements. Indeed, the ACA membership as a group had nothing to do with radical women who were active in suffrage movements. Unlike these more radical spokeswomen who talked of equality between the sexes, most college women spoke instead of accommodating their education to the "natural" inclinations of their sex. If higher education had once had the potential to contribute to a radical philosophy of goals for women, it now was fostering more conservative views. It seems that the ACA was willing to trade its own potential radicalism for a modest extension of legitimate roles for women, and that educational diplomas were becoming occupational credentials as they had never been in the nineteenth century.

To some extent, the distribution of membership was determining the degree of support for these new courses and careers—and, thus, for this conservative outlook. The smaller, eastern women's colleges had been dominant in an era when "mere culture" had positive connotations. But the larger coeducational institutions had much more diversity of courses and, generally, because of a disparate population as well as the trend toward utility in undergraduate education, stressed specialization. For women, specialized courses usually meant home economics. Spokesmen from these large universities confirmed the importance of particularized training. Dr. Calvin M. Woodward, then dean of the specialized School of Engineering at Washington University and early exponent of "progressive" educational reforms, told the ACA convention in 1905 that "I have great hopes for schools of domestic science and household art. The girl whose school training leads her to look with contempt upon homely duties . . . is not rationally taught." [33] R. H. Jesse, president of the University of Missouri, chided those colleges who had still not offered courses in household economy. "All colleges and universities that admit women should recognize the fact, that the majority of their pupils will marry and ought to do so." [34] Charles Richard Van Hise, president of the University of Wisconsin, talked also of the "natural segregation" of professional courses—engineering, agriculture, and commerce for men, and home economics for women.[35] The smaller women's colleges—Bryn Mawr, Vassar, Smith, Mount Holyoke, Barnard, Radcliffe, Wellesley, Sophie Newcomb College, the Women's College of Baltimore, and Western Reserve Annex—had not yet offered these courses. Before too long most of these schools would also follow suit.

Those who attended the 1908 national convention saw a most distinguished parade of visitors. George Herbert Palmer spoke of his wife's desire for college-educated women to care for the sick, poor, and feeble of society and praised the membership for heeding her call.[36] William James addressed the assembly about the social value of the college-bred woman. Their activities could give assurance that public welfare was not collapsing with the advance of industry.[37] And Charles Eliot praised not only the college woman's desire to use her education for social reformist purposes, but also her willingness to give more narrowly defined domestic concerns her true priority. In an address which twenty years before might have met with harsh reactions, Eliot began by saying that it had been proven that women could handle "men's" studies; therefore, women's colleges were now free to arrange for education adapted to the needs of women, which related primarily to the greatest single occupation—the raising of children: "The one great occupation for women is the most intellectual occupation there is in the world. It calls, and calls loudly, and often calls in vain, for carefully trained mental powers, as well as great moral powers. . . . I look forward therefore to the future of the higher education for women as a great influence in the perfecting of home life, of family life, of household joy and good." [38]

The "ambitious" women leaders like Carey Thomas, who tried to make women's education commensurate with men's, were no longer outspoken since "ambition" had come to be more compatible with widely accepted occupations for educated women. Clearly, Eliot was pleased by this development. Women like Carey Thomas must have cringed at Eliot's implication that intellectual studies were only for men. But the bulk of the membership loudly applauded; despite their new professionalized careers, they had heeded the call to make intellectuality subservient to domesticity. At that same meeting, Laura Drake Gill, Barnard's president as well as president of the ACA from 1907 to 1911, urged her membership to embrace social service avocations for they were "not contrary to the social interests of women." She went on to say: "The fact that the number of women is not increasing markedly in the older professions of law, medicine, and theology seems to indicate that other service is better adapted to the exigencies of woman's racial position and to her taste than are they." [39]

Thus, the social service occupations might satisfy the college woman who was torn between domesticity and a desire to make use of her special preparation. ACA women stressed that traditional woman's work was now spreading to a larger, more complex arena. Housekeeping would not stop at the threshold but would continue into the dusty, insect-infested streets and public buildings. Frederick Henry Sykes, president of the Connecticut College for Women, wrote in 1917: "Women must still make the individual home; we must count on them also to make the larger home, to civilize the city." [40]

By the beginning of World War I, social service work had become not a mere vocational option for college women but a *responsibility*. Articles and speeches urged women to make the special kinds of contributions that society needed and that women were specifically gifted to furnish. The coming of the war made service occupations particularly vital, and extended the concepts of providing order and tranquillity into the armed forces. In 1917 a resolution was passed in the annual meeting of the ACA: "Resolved that we . . . unreservedly place ourselves at the disposal of the President and the Government of the U.S. for any form of service which we may be able to render in the present crisis. . . ." Interestingly, the kinds of services offered as examples of those college women might provide were all of a domestic nature. In addition to providing comfortable, sanitary conditions for homes and cities, women might now do the same for the fighting men. They might supervise food selection and the distribution of food, supplies, "safeguard the leisure hours of our young men," and "surround them with the normal conditions of living." [41]

Not all college women, of course, pursued a career in social work or concentrated full-time on perfecting their household arts. There was a great diversity of life style and occupation among educated women. However, the great rhetorical emphasis placed upon service and domestic occupations and the rationales put forth by ACA women suggest a great need to find ways in which they could remain within the limits of domestic ideology and still justify their college education. Although it was never clear specifically how collegiate education could give a larger significance to the traditional woman's sphere, the fact remained that women now had, at the very least, a new set of terms to describe domestic work, and, in some cases, new technical knowledge to apply. Women might now use their education to manage the home as if it were a new industry—the woman's monopoly.

NOTES

1. Quoted in Marion Talbot and Lois Kimball Mathews Rosenberry, *The History of the American Association of University Women 1881–1931* (Boston, 1931), p. 14. Talbot was one of the founders of the ACA, and her book is a compilation of information about the organization. Words of praise are constantly interjected

among the mass of facts about committees, local branches, sponsored research, and so on.

2. Helen Hiscock Backus, "Some Recent Phases in the Development of American Colleges," *ACA Publications*, Series II, No. 17 (May 1889).

From 1882 to 1898 the ACA issued scattered publications. After 1888 numbering of printed issues began with Series II. Only with Series III, beginning in 1898, did publications appear in magazine form, and a more orderly arrangement began. From January 1911 on, the publications were issued in a journal with regular volume and issue numbers.

3. An example of some titles (which speak for themselves): F. C. Taylor, "Effects in Woman of Imperfect Hygiene of Sex Functions," *American Journal of Obstetrics,* 1882; T. S. Clouston, "Female Education from a Medical Point of View, *Popular Science Monthly,* 1884; "Education and Race Suicide," *American Journal of Heredity,* 1890.

4. Annie G. Howes, Chairman, "Health Status of College Graduates," *ACA Publications* (1885).

5. Many of these authors were also members of the ACA. For example: Anna Brackett's "Liberal Education for Women," *Harper's,* 1877; Helen Hiscock Backus's "Should the College Train for Motherhood?," *Outlook,* February 1899; Millicent Shinn's "Marriage-Rate of College Women," *Century,* October 1895.

6. G. Stanley Hall, *Adolescence—Its Psychology and its Relations to Physiology, Anthropology, Sociology, Sex, Crime, Religion and Education,* Vol. 2 (New York, 1904), p. 634.

7. See, for example, A. Lapthon Smith's "Higher Education of Women and Race Suicide," *Popular Science Monthly* (March 1905). This article has the typical scathing generalizations about college women: that they make very poor mothers and that they have caused the gradual disappearance of the home. The *Popular Science Monthly* printed a response to the Smith article by a college woman, Olivia R. Fernon ("Does Higher Education Unfit Women for Motherhood?," April 1905). Typically, she did not condemn Smith's thesis, but called it "very interesting" and went on to say that women ought to *reform* education to make it more in tune with demands of a domestic life.

8. This was happening particularly at the University of Chicago and the University of Wisconsin between 1900 and 1905.

9. Richard J. Storr, *Harper's University—The Beginnings* (Chicago, 1966), p. 306.

10. Abby Leach, "The Ideal Curriculum for a Woman's College," *ACA Publications,* Series III, No. 2 (December 1898).

11. Mary Roberts Smith, "Shall the College Curriculum Be Modified for Women," *ACA Publications,* Series III, No. 1 (December 1898).

12. David Potter has written that just as the wilderness may have been a frontier for American men, "the city was the frontier for American women." While he was referring specifically to the opportunities for women to work in clerical positions in business offices, it is no less true that the city was also an arena for social reform. And this latter field also provided a way to link rhetorically new opportunities with old expectations for women. (See David

Potter, "American Women and the American Character," in *History and American Society, Essays of David M. Potter* (New York, 1973), pp. 277–304.

13. Kate Holladay Claghorn, "The Problem of Occupation for College Women," *ACA Publications*, Series II, No. 21 (1897).

14. "Compensation in Certain Occupations of Women Who Have Received College or Other Special Training," *ACA Publications*, Series II, No. 12 (1897).

15. Helen Hiscock Backus, "The Need and the Opportunity for College Trained Women in Philanthropic Work," *ACA Publications*, Series II, No. 17 (March 1887).

16. Vida Scudder, "The Relation of College Women to Social Need," *ACA Publications*, Series II, No. 30 (1890).

17. Millicent W. Shinn, "Baby's Mind," *ACA Publications*, Series II, No. 52 (1894).

18. Ellen H. Richards, "The Relation of College Women to Progress in Domestic Science," *ACA Publications*, Series II, No. 27 (1890).

19. Annie Howes Barus, "The College Woman's Opportunity in Cooperative Work," *ACA Publications*, Series III, No. 1 (December 1898).

20. The NEA wished to secure greater elasticity in college entrance requirements, while the ACA was averse to having the college yield on any area of its control—including the crucial aspect of determining entrance requirements.

21. Record of the annual meeting in Denver, January 1911, ACA *Journal* 4: 18.

22. Susan M. Kingsbury, "Economic Efficiency of the College Woman," *ACA Publications*, Series III, No. 17 (1908).

23. Talbott, p. 177.

24. The only exception to this, according to ACA publications, was money given to the fellowship committee by Judge James B. Bradwell of Chicago when his daughter, Mrs. Bessie Bradwell Helmer, was chairwoman.

25. William R. Harper, address of welcome at the February 1900 meeting of the ACA, *ACA Publications*, Series III, No. 3 (1900).

26. By 1905 the sex segregation in the Junior College at the University of Chicago was complete. Different residential colleges were created, some of which were exclusively for men and others exclusively for women. Although the faculty was divided over the issue, Harper was in favor of it as was Albion Small, an influential faculty member. When Small was president of Colby College in 1890, he had proposed the institution of coordinate colleges for men and women. See Storr, pp. 325–27.

27. Lefavour's university affiliation is unclear. He was referred to, though, by the title of "professor."

28. Henry Lefavour, "The Utilitarian in Higher Education," *ACA Publications*, Series III, No. 6 (1903).

29. Welcome address by the president of the Washington Branch at the 1903 annual meeting, *ACA Publications*, Series III, no. 6 (1903).

30. May S. Cheney, "Will Nature Eliminate the College Woman," *ACA Publications*, Series III, No. 10 (1905).

31. Charles Richmond Henderson, "Professional Education for Social Service," *ACA Publications*, Series III, No. 9 (1904).

32. Edward T. Devine, "The Economic Place of Women," *ACA Publications,* Series III, No. 9 (1904). Devine repeated this same theme in other forums with few changes in words. His speech, for example, before the American Academy of Political and Social Science, entitled "The Economic Function of Women," worked the same ideas. See *Annals of the American Academy of Political and Social Science* 5 (July 1894–June 1895).

33. Dr. C. M. Woodward, address of welcome at the annual meeting of the ACA, *ACA Publications,* Series III, No. 10 (1905).

34. R. H. Jesse, "The Position of Household Economics in the Academic Curriculum," *ACA Publications,* Series III, No. 10 (1905).

35. Charles Richard Van Hise, "Educational Tendencies in State Universities," *ACA Publications,* Series III, no. 17 (1908).

36. George Herbert Palmer, "The Contribution of Alice Freeman Palmer to the Upholding of the Association," *ACA Publications,* Series III, No. 17 (1908).

37. William James, "The Social Value of the College-Bred Woman," *ACA Publications,* Series III, No. 17 (1908).

38. Charles Eliot, "Women's Education: A Forecast," *ACA Publications,* Series III, No. 17 (1908).

39. Laura Drake Gill, address of welcome at the meeting in 1908, *ACA Publications,* Series III, No. 18 (1908).

40. Frederick Henry Sykes, "The Social Basis of the New Education for Women," *Teachers College Record* 18 (May 1917): 240.

41. Resolution contained in minutes of 1917 annual meeting of the ACA, *ACA Journal* 10 (May 1917).

EPILOGUE

Ellen H. Richards and the
New Professional Education for Women

Ellen H. Richards was perhaps the prime spokesperson within the Association of Collegiate Alumnae for new careers for educated women. She is a prototype for those who, by 1910, saw careers in social and domestic reform as a way of contributing to higher living standards and also as a way of bringing professional stature to traditional woman's work. Her particular bents were sanitary science and household economy. She went to college at Vassar and then, as the Massachusetts Institute of Technology's first woman student, specialized in chemistry. Richards spread the social service through science gospel tirelessly throughout her later life, not only in the ACA but also in the Home Economics Association, which she founded almost singlehandedly. The titles of some of her numerous publications speak for themselves: *The Chemistry of Cooking and Cleaning* and *Food Materials and their Adulteration.*

Richards was admitted to MIT in 1870 as a special student in chemistry after much administrative deliberation. The college intended no such radical change in admissions policy, however, as is seen by the resolution of the faculty after agreeing to admit Miss Richards: *"Resolved* That the Faculty are of the opinion that the admission of women as special students is as yet in the nature of an experiment, that each application should be acted on upon its own merits, and that no general action or change of the former policy of the Institution is at present expedient." [1] Ellen Richards's association with MIT lasted until her death in 1911. She eventually became an instructor in sanitary chemistry. Having succeeded in entering an exclusionary institution, Richards in 1876 set up the Woman's Laboratory, an alternative structure within MIT's domain—although not part of the regular academic program—where women might obtain scientific training.

For Richards the conflict between intellectuality and domesticity was never really a problem; she had resolved it by finding a niche for herself that compromised neither her sense of womanliness nor her academic training. Yet the resolution bred a conservative approach to the question of appropriate roles for educated women, and her position was filled with inconsistencies and problems that later generations of women, trying to follow her lead, would eventually confront. To begin with, Richards, in attempting to place home economics on an equal footing with other newly touted applied sciences such as engineering, was making a false comparison. Because home economy—and even social service work—were seen as inherently feminine, they would not easily attain the stature of men's work. And, more important, many women would never be paid for work in home economy or in social service. As Carol Lopate points out in an article entitled "The Irony of the Home Economics Movement":

> The ideology of home economics sought to upgrade the status of women's work by employing language and linguistic distinctions which applied to the world of business and industry. But no books on the subject questioned the lack of parallels between the home and industry which the ideology obscured. None mentioned the pay/no pay distinction, and none mentioned the isolation of women at home which did not apply to men (or women) in factories and offices. [2]

Such issues as nonpayment were never a reality for Richards. She was always in the mainstream of academia and held important positions in many organizations. Her biographer, Caroline Hunt, has said of her that "There can be no doubt that she loved power, and had a pleasurable interest in all its manifestations. . . ." [3] Why then, one wonders, did she espouse positions for women that inevitably promoted inequality? One striking example of the inconsistency between her own life and the opportunities she was willing to endorse for other educated women concerns her position on the question of admission of women to MIT on an equal status with men. She herself had fought to gain entry, albeit as a special student; yet in 1878, when women were admitted on exactly the same footing as men, "Mrs. Richards was not fully in sympathy. She believed that it would be wiser not to admit them until the third year. She was overruled, and wisely perhaps, but her objections, though based on an enthusiastic overestimate of the demand for scientific education, were very characteristic of her attitude of mind." [4] She seemed much more disposed to having women continue to attend her Woman's Laboratory, which offered scientific training with second-class status.

Richards's position on women's rights—particularly suffrage—was equally injurious to the future status of women. Her statements on the subject sound extremely condescending: "I sympathize with father and I wish the women's rights folks would be more sensible. I think the women have a great deal to learn, before they are fit to vote." [5] On another occasion she said: "Women have now more rights and duties than they are fitted to perform. They need to measure themselves with men on the same terms and in the same work in order to learn their own needs." [6] Interestingly, she did not stop to realize that her own aspirations for women included doing work that was very specifically suited for *women*. Also interesting is the fact that, in using the pronoun "they" to describe women, she seems to exclude herself from the group entirely. And she often did—finding a constant need in her life to be special: "You will know that one of my delights is to do something that no one else ever did. I have the chance of doing what no woman ever did. . . ." [7]

In doing what no woman ever did (entering the Massachusetts Institute of Technology) she realized very clearly that her conservative approach to the questions of women's rights helped her to gain access to men's spheres. Her awareness of this point is indicated in a revealing statement written in a letter after her acceptance to MIT: "Perhaps the fact that I am not a Radical or a believer in the all powerful ballot for women to right her wrongs and that I do not scorn womanly duties, but claim it as a privilege to clean up and sort of sew things, etc., is winning me stronger allies than anything else." [8]

The dichotomy between Richards's personal strivings and her aspirations for college-educated women is reminiscent of a similar division in Alice Freeman Palmer's life. Palmer's enjoyment of her powerful position and her desire to attain a special stature is more understated than Richards's but existed nevertheless. Her statements about Wellesley college graduates being suited particularly for home and charitable occupations were not as defined as Richards's scientific, professional careers; yet the arenas were the same.

Both Palmer and Richards came from fairly poor families in rural areas—Palmer from western New York, Richards from northern Massachusetts. Their mothers had both been schoolteachers; their fathers groped throughout their lives for an occupation that would enable them to support their families comfortably. Both Palmer and Richards were extremely energetic—helping their families earn a livelihood while simultaneously excelling in the village school. Neither could bear inactivity. For Richards "inactivity" meant housework, work in her father's store, in the church, and in the Sunday school, work that was not commensurate with her ambition and that caused her considerable suffering: ". . . the unused energy within her seems fairly to have turned upon her and to have reduced her almost to a condition of invalidism." [9] She would later try to encourage college women to engage in similar pursuits by making them more palatable. Palmer and Richards saw escape in the new opportunity for women to attend college; Palmer went to the University of Michigan in 1872, and Richards attended Vassar in 1868. Both women went on to achieve prominence in academia; they were colleagues in the Association of Collegiate Alumnae. Palmer took a class in the MIT Woman's Laboratory when it first started, and, in 1884, they traveled together to the International Health Exhibition in England.

But for Palmer the dichotomy between her own ambition and her stated preferences for her college students (and, thus, for the ideal educated woman) caused her to undergo a personal crisis which resulted in her leaving Wellesley and marrying George Herbert Palmer. Ellen Richards also married late in life; but her marriage did not in any way interfere with her professional life. The differences reflect, in part, their differing academic roles and the nature of the institution to which they were affiliated.

The conflict between intellect and domesticity was never resolved satisfactorily for Alice Palmer at Wellesley. As president she was keenly aware that Wellesley's curriculum was based solely on the liberal arts; it was not conceived of as a college that would prepare graduates for specific professional or technical careers. Like other new women's colleges, Wellesley sought to emulate the rigor of the best of the men's liberal arts institutions. But whereas many men, upon leaving under-graduate institutions, attended professional graduate schools, women most often terminated their education after undergraduate work. Career plans were formulated amidst the amorphous liberal arts course offerings. Alice Palmer, as president of Wellesley, had to articulate goals for college women. Her suggestions reveal an attempt to combine traditional views of women with an intellectual training. The results were statements praising graduates with exceptional careers in such areas as law and medicine along with vague pronouncements about how the college woman's heightened sensitivity would aid her work with children, with the sick, and with the downtrodden. The lack of definition did not help her resolve her own conflict. Her situation was made more difficult because her role as college president made her especially susceptible to public scrutiny; she was the symbol of Wellesley College and could not unravel her ambivalences in private. In addition, for George Herbert Palmer, the idea that her influential position could coexist with a marriage was close to preposterous. In the end she was forced to make a clear choice between marriage—with a variety of social service activities attached—and career.

Ellen Richards never had to make such a choice. Her professional responsibilities meshed well with her private life. As an advocate of very distinct and defined careers for women, Richards was always clear in her thoughts about roles for female college graduates. Domestic economy could be practiced in a woman's own kitchen; she, herself, saw her own home as a model for the incorporation of scientific management, and frequently entertained students so that they might see firsthand the practical outcomes of their study. Her thoroughness as a household manager was unchallengeable:

> When Mrs. Richards began housekeeping in the seventies, she furnished her house with carpets as everyone else did. But when for the sake of greater convenience or safety she changed her methods; when, for example, she substituted rugs for carpets, began to use gas instead of coal for cooking, installed a telephone, or experimented with the vacuum cleaner for house cleaning, she always counted the cost, not only in money, but in time and steps. When she began to use a gas stove she had a meter placed in her kitchen, and with the assistance of a young engineer who was living in her home made a thorough study of the amount of gas required for preparing difference dishes and for carrying on various household processes. She carefully computed, too, the amount of time involved in caring for rugs and hardwood floors as compared with carpets.[10]

She proselytized what she lived, minimizing any conflict that she might feel about her career. Both she and her husband were on the faculty at MIT—he specialized in mining engineering, and, as professor, held a higher position than she. Yet they respected each other's work and apparently were supportive of and encouraging to one other.

Richards's success at MIT and her lack of conflict about her career in general is definitely related to the type of study that she was engaged in and her ideas about women's role as "missionaries to a suffering humanity." [11] She defined socially acceptable ways for a woman to use her education: running her home more efficiently, becoming involved in health and sanitary problems in schools in particular, or engaging in various charitable pursuits. And her speeches—primarily before the Association of Collegiate Alumnae—were converting more and more people to the idea that women needed to strive for such "suitable" careers; the pure liberal arts curriculum was far too unspecific, causing too many women to grope for ways of making themselves useful. As early as 1890 she advocated the study of domestic economy in all colleges for women. The college must, she thought, maintain the dignity of woman's home sphere. Richards typically kept the larger picture in mind as well when she said that domestic economy would "broaden the ideas of life with which the young woman leaves college, . . . [and] bring her in touch with the great problems which press more closely each year." Also, the study would "secure a solid basis for improvement. Those of us who had a hand in reforms know how much work is wasted for want of knowing what has already been done." [12] Interestingly, Richards did not always hold such a strong position with respect to specialization. While a student at Vassar in 1868 she wrote: "I do not intend to ever say anything in reply to the half sarcastic inquiries and covert sneers I have heard so much from those who think that a person must have a profession if she has been to college. College is a place to learn. When you find the stuff you are made of, then is the time to choose and study a profession, if ever." [13]

Richards's conversion was perhaps more dramatic than others; but it nonetheless was indicative of changing thoughts on the subject. The increased influence of growing state universities, with their ability to offer diverse course ranges, promoted specialization. Liberal arts education did not, of course, disappear. Yet the prevailing attitudes about the function of a college education for women bred a more limited outlook in the liberal arts colleges (many of which began to offer specialized courses) and insured that some separation of the sexes because of course preference was occurring at the larger coeducational universities.

A few women involved in higher education remained advocates of the pure liberal arts curricula for women students; as late as 1918 Carey Thomas called for a return to the "old fashioned disciplines." She felt that specialized education for women—anything from sanitary science to domestic science to child study—would be disastrous for the whole concept of women's higher education.[14] She eventually gave in to the extent that Bryn Mawr offered courses in social work on the graduate level; most were theoretically rather than practically oriented, yet their existence represented some change in Thomas's thinking.

By 1910 women involved in higher education—at least those who were members of the ACA—saw colleges as a way of insuring that traditional woman's work would take on a larger significance. The home would no longer be "swept bare of its interesting occupations. . . ." [15] The institutional setting, by forcing women to confront the question of intellectuality versus domesticity, seems to have insured a clinging to traditional values, placed in a frame of professionalism.

It was outside of the institutional educational settings that real alternatives for women were either articulated most vehemently or acted out. The late nineteenth and early twentieth century was a period in which women sought to win political equality. It is significant that the Association of Collegiate Alumnae, the representative body of college women, never endorsed or participated in this struggle. Women's education throughout the nineteenth century had sought to prepare women to carry out their "natural bents" more effectively; colleges, at least in their beginning years, never succeeded in offering a real alternative to this type of preparation.

NOTES

1. Quoted in Carolyn L. Hunt, *The Life of Ellen H. Richards* (Washington, D.C., 1958), p. 41.

2. Carol Lopate, "The Irony of the Home Economics Movement," *Edcentric: A Journal of Educational Change* (November 1974): 56.

3. Hunt, p. 183.

4. Ibid., p. 77.

5. Letter from Ellen H. Richards to her parents, March 13, 1870, quoted in Hunt, p. 194.

6. Quoted in Hunt, p. 159.

7. Letter from Ellen H. Richards to unknown recipient on December 25, 1870, quoted in Hunt, p. 42.

8. Quoted in Janet Wilson James, "Ellen H. Richards," in *Notable American Women*, ed. Edward T. James, vol. 3 (Cambridge, Mass., 1971).

9. Hunt, p. 21.

10. Ibid., pp. 59–60.

11. Ibid., p. 55.

12. Ellen H. Richards, "The Relation of College Women to Progress in Domestic Science," *ACA Publications*, Series II, No. 27 (1890).

13. Letter from Ellen H. Richards to her parents, May 16, 1869, quoted in Hunt, p. 33.

14. Martha Carey Thomas, "Present Tendencies in Women's College and University Education," *Educational Review* 25 (1908).

15. Ellen H. Richards, "The Relation of College Women to Progress in Domestic Science."

Appendix

TABLE 1
Advanced Study of
Women Graduates of the University of Michigan, [1,2]
1889–1908

Classes of	1889–93	1894–98	1899–1903	1904–8	Total
Advanced study					
MA	41–18%	57–15%	77–13%	84–11%	249–13%
PhD	9– 4%	10– 3%	7– 1%	8– 1%	34– 2%
MD or LLB	12– 6%	5– 1%	10– 2%	11– 1%	38– 2%
BS or RN	3– 1%	3– 1%	4– 1%	5– 1%	15– 1%
Advanced study/No degree	1– 1%	4– 1%	22– 4%	28– 4%	55– 3%
Subtotal	66–30%	72–21%	120–21%	136–18%	391–21%
No advanced study	152–71%	326–79%	488–79%	614–82%	1583–79%
Total sample	218	398	608	750	1974

[1] based upon the total population of University of Michigan women graduates taken from University of Michigan alumnae registers.

[2] In cases where alumnae received two degrees, the more advanced one was recorded.

TABLE 2

Occupations of Women Graduates of
the University of Michigan,
1889–1908 [1]

Classes of	1889–93	1894–98	1899–1903	1904–8	Total
Teaching/ tutoring	36–17%	100–25%	148–24%	189–25%	473–24%
College teaching	12– 6%	8– 2%	15– 2%	13– 2%	48– 2%
Clerical work	—	6– 2%	4– 1%	5– 1%	15– 1%
Social work	—	3– 1%	2–	11– 1%	16– 1%
Librarian	1–	9– 2%	9– 1%	12– 2%	31– 1%
Doctor, lawyer	4– 2%	3– 1%	6– 1%	6– 1%	19– 1%
Other [2]	9– 4%	18– 5%	24– 4%	31– 4%	82– 4%
None	156–71%	251–62%	400–67%	483–64%	1290–66%
Total sample	218	398	608	750	1974

[1] based upon the total population of University of Michigan women graduates taken from University of Michigan alumnae registers.

[2] Occupations in the "other" category are more easily summarized than specified. The most frequent are: writers, editors, farmers, missionaries, and scientific technicians.

TABLE 3

Marriage Rates of Women Graduates of
the University of Michigan,
1889–1908 [1],[2]

Classes of	1889–93	1894–98	1899–1903	1904–8	Total
Married	118–55%	199–50%	328–54%	386–52%	1031–53%
Unmarried	100–45%	199–50%	320–46%	364–48%	943–47%
Total sample	218	398	608	750	1974

[1] based upon the total population of University of Michigan women graduates taken from University of Michigan alumnae registers.

[2] Statistics for these graduates were taken through 1923 because the alumnae register for graduates from these years only goes up to that year.

TABLE 4
Comparison of Marriage Rates for Women Graduates of the University of Michigan, 1889–1908 and 1909–18 [1]

	1889–1908	1909–18 [2]	Total
Married	1031–53%	1171–60%	2202–56%
Unmarried	943–47%	781–40%	1724–44%
Total sample	1974	1952	3926

[1] based upon a total sample of women graduates of the University of Michigan taken from alumnae registers.

[2] It is crucial to point out that these later statistics (1909–18) are not completely accurate because the alumnae register for early graduates was published in 1925. It may be assumed, therefore, that marriage rates for graduates from 1909 to 1918 were higher than 60 percent—they probably surpassed those for Bryn Mawr which were 67 percent for the same period. Also, they most likely did not surpass the rates for Wellesley graduates during that period, which were 72 percent. Therefore, it is fairly safe to assume that the rates for Michigan students fell somewhere in the middle of the two women's colleges. This is similar to the pattern for the previous period from 1889 to 1908.

TABLE 5

Comparison of Advanced Study
for Women Graduates of
The University of Michigan,
1889–1908
and 1909–18 [1,2]

Classes of	1889–1908	1909–18 [3]	Total
Advanced study			
MA	249–13%	273–14%	522–13%
PhD	34– 2%	2–	36– 1%
MD or LLB	38– 2%	12– 1%	50– 1%
BS or RN	15– 1%	12– 1%	27– 1%
Advanced study/No degree	55– 3%	116– 6%	171– 4%
Subtotal	391–21%	415–22%	806–20%
No advanced study	1583–79%	1537–78%	3120–79%
Total sample	1974	1952	3926

[1] based upon a total population of women graduates of the University of Michigan taken from alumnae registers.

[2] In cases where alumnae received two degrees, the more advanced one was recorded.

[3] Again, as in Table 4, it is important to point out that these later statistics (1909–18) are not completely accurate because the alumnae register for early graduates was published in 1925. It may be assumed that more students pursued advanced study than is indicated on this table—particularly with reference to PhD, MD, and LLB degrees. It also may be assumed that rates for the University of Michigan remained below those for both Bryn Mawr and Wellesley.

TABLE 6
Comparison of Occupations
for Women Graduates of
the University of Michigan,
1889–1908
and 1909–18 [1]

	1889–1908	1909–18	Total
Teaching/ tutoring	473–24%	495–25%	968–25%
College teaching	48– 2%	18– 1%	66– 2%
Clerical work	15– 1%	35– 2%	50– 1%
Social work	16– 1%	45– 2%	61– 2%
Librarian	31– 1%	32– 2%	63– 2%
Doctor, lawyer	19– 1%	9–	28– 1%
Other [2]	82– 4%	69– 4%	151– 4%
None	1290–66%	1249–64%	2539–65%
Total sample	1974	1952	3926

[1] based upon a total sample of women graduates of the University of Michigan taken from alumnae registers.

[2] Because there are 151 occupations in the "other" category, these occupations are more easily summarized than specified. There are similarities in this category for both time periods. The most frequent occupations are: writers, reporters, editors, farmers, missionaries, and scientific and research assistants.

Index